# Life-Changing Bible Studies From the New Testament

Loveland, Colorado

## Life-Changing Bible Studies From the New Testament

Copyright © 1992 Group Publishing, Inc.
First Printing

### Credits

Edited by Michael Warden and Lois Keffer
Cover designed by Jean Bruns
Book designed by Dori Walker

### Contributors

Many thanks to the following authors who contributed their expertise to create this collection:
Mike Gillespie
Stephen Parolini
Annie Wamberg
Steve Wamberg
Michael Warden
Gary Wilde
Paul Woods

### Library of Congress Cataloging-in-Publication Data

Life-changing Bible studies from the New Testament / [edited by Michael Warden].
    p.   cm.
    ISBN 1-55945-079-7
    1. Bible. N.T.--Study and teaching.   2. Teenagers--Religious life.
I. Warden, Michael D.
BS2408.L54 1992
225.6--dc20

                          92-16
                          CIP

Printed in the United States of America

# C • O • N • T • E • N • T • S

## Life-Changing Bible Studies From the New Testament

The New Testament reveals God's ultimate answer to human sin. It is the complete revelation of Jesus Christ—from his times as a man on earth, to the revelation of his Spirit in his church, to the eternal life that comes from his life in us today. Through the New Testament, we not only learn who Jesus is and what he is like, we also discover how we can know him personally and grow to be like him in our own lives. It truly is the "greatest story ever told."

Each generation faces the challenge of conveying the messages of the New Testament to its children. Today more than ever, kids hunger for the truth found in the pages of God's Word. But how do we help kids digest the wealth of truth found in the New Testament? How do we help them understand the New Testament's relevance to their lives? *Life-Changing Bible Studies From the New Testament* uses five principles that help open the doors to understanding and application in kids' lives.

● **Principle 1: Present God's Word.** Kids need to wrestle directly with scripture. Each session in this book lets kids dig into a specific passage and discover its meaning. The scriptures are never watered down. Rather, each session's goal is to let the Holy Spirit use the scripture to deepen kids' understanding of God's ways.

● **Principle 2: Help kids relate God's Word to their lives.** Teenagers need to see a correlation between the teachings of the New Testament and their lives. To bridge this gap, each session includes an Experience section to bring kids to a deeper understanding of how the passage applies to their lives.

● **Principle 3: Let the Holy Spirit work.** It's God's Holy Spirit that empowers young people and brings them to "aha!" times of discovery. By creating an atmosphere where God can work, we enable kids to learn more than we could ever teach them on our own. Each session allows kids a critical debriefing time, which opens the door for the Holy Spirit to lead kids toward new discoveries about God and themselves.

● **Principle 4: Show kids the "big picture."** This book high-lights the entire New Testament. Why? Because only after you wrestle with all the pieces can you understand how the puzzle fits together. Kids want to know how the whole New Testament fits together. They need to see the connection between Jesus and Paul, or between Peter and John, for example.

● **Principle 5: Use a variety of learning experiences.** Using the same learning approach week after week dulls your kids' inter-est. In this book, each session's approach differs slightly from the rest. In one session, kids explore the difference between faith and law by creating plaster-of-Paris molds. In another, kids learn about the cost of discipleship by acting out a humorous drama. Using variety in learning experiences keeps kids coming back for more.

# ◆ How to Prepare for These Studies

Combined with your leadership skills and a few simple sup-plies, *Life-Changing Bible Studies From the New Testament* pro-vides everything you need to lead effective and creative Bible studies that will help kids learn from the New Testament.

Each session contains a brief overview of the topic and pas-sage and gives a detailed list of the supplies you'll need to lead the session.

As you prepare for each session, make sure you study the cen-tral passage so you can help kids stretch toward an understanding that goes beneath the surface. Also, pray for your kids while you do these studies. Ask the Holy Spirit to lead them toward greater understanding and practical applications of the things they learn. Invite God to work through you as you lead these sessions.

*Life-Changing Bible Studies From the New Testament* makes the New Testament come alive for teenagers. The sessions teach and confront kids where they are. They examine kids' beliefs and lifestyles. Use this collection of studies to enable your teenagers to grow in their knowledge of God's grace and love for them.

# Who Do You Say That I Am?

## ◆ Theme: Survey of the Gospels

The four gospels anchor the New Testament. They contain the history of the life, death and resurrection of Jesus Christ. Their title—gospel—means "good news." And that was their intended purpose: to present the saving legacy of God's Son.

Most teenagers grow up getting bits and pieces of the gospels. Few have read and studied them at length. Yet, kids need the information presented in the gospels to grow in their faith.

This session surveys Matthew, Mark, Luke and John to help kids get a balanced picture of Jesus' ministry. The session will lead kids to new discoveries about Jesus and his role in their lives today.

## ◆ Objectives

During this session kids will:
● review events from Jesus' life;
● survey the four gospels;
● re-enact a part of Jesus' life; and
● commit to reading one of the gospels.

## ◆ Preparation

Read and study highlights of the four gospels.
Gather a ball of yarn, Bibles, 3×5 cards and pencils.

# The Session

## ◆ Dig

Welcome students and have them sit in a tight circle. Say: **Today we're going to explore the ministry of Jesus found in the Gospels of Matthew, Mark, Luke and John. Think for a moment about Jesus' life. How much can you remember?**

Hold up the ball of yarn and say: **I'm going to tie this yarn to my finger and throw it to another person in the circle. When you catch it, wrap it around your finger and tell the group one event or fact from Jesus' life. For example, you might say he was born in a manger or he once healed a blind man. Then throw the yarn to another person in the circle, keeping one end of the yarn wrapped around your finger. No event can be repeated.**

Begin passing the yarn. Gradually you'll form a web of yarn among students. When kids begin to run out of events they remember, ask:

● **What do you think of the web we've created here?**

● **How is this web like the collective knowledge we have about Christ's life?**

● **How is this web like your own personal knowledge of Christ?**

Say: **A web is only as strong as the number of strands it contains. In the same way, the more truth we have about Christ in our hearts, the stronger our faith becomes. That's why the gospels are so important. They contain vital information about Jesus. Without the gospels we can't really understand who Jesus is or what he came to earth to do.**

## ◆ Discover

Say: **Let's play a game to find out how many truths we can discover about Jesus.**

Form teams of about five. Give each person a Bible. Be sure

each team has at least one Bible with a concordance. Point out the concordance and the location of the gospels.

Say: **I'm going to read a series of fill-in-the-blank statements one at a time. The first team to answer a question correctly will send one of its members over to me. That person will stay with me for the remainder of the game. If the answering team can also read a scripture passage supporting the correct answer, that team can send an additional person to me. The first team to run out of people wins.**

Have teams form small circles, with their Bibles ready. Instruct teams to indicate they have an answer by having one person raise his or her hand. Read the following questions, pausing to let groups find the answers. Continue until one team runs out of people.

Possible answers are listed in a box on page 10. Kids may come up with correct answers or references that are different from the ones in the box. Accept any answers kids can support from the Bible.

Play two rounds if you have enough time and questions.

1. The teachers in the Temple were _____ by Jesus as a boy.

2. When tempted by Satan, Jesus answered by _____ _____.

3. After calming the storm, Jesus questioned his disciples' _____.

4. Jesus said, "I am the _____ and the _____ and the _____."

5. Jesus said you are the _____ of the earth and the _____ of the world.

6. Jesus told us to _____ our enemies.

7. After Jesus healed his blindness, Bartimaeus _____ _____.

8. When they heard about Jesus' raising Lazarus from the dead, the Pharisees were afraid everyone would _____.

9. When Jesus first saw his disciples after his resurrection, he greeted them by saying, "_____!"

10. Jesus once fed thousands of people with _____ and _____.

11. Jesus said his true brothers and sisters are _____.

12. Jesus told us to become like _____ if we want to enter the kingdom of heaven.

13. Jesus said the two greatest commandments are _____ _____ and _____.

14. While on the cross, Jesus asked one of his disciples to take care of Jesus' _____.

15. At Jesus' trial, Herod was _____ when he saw Jesus.

---

# ANSWERS

1. amazed (Luke 2:47)
2. quoting scripture (Luke 4:1-12)
3. faith (Luke 8:22-25)
4. way, truth, life (John 14:6)
5. salt, light (Matthew 5:13-14)
6. love (Matthew 5:44)
7. followed Jesus (Mark 10:52)
8. believe in Jesus (John 11:43-48)
9. Peace be with you (John 20:19)
10. five loaves of bread, two small fish (Mark 6:5-13)
11. people who do God's will (Matthew 12:50)
12. children (Matthew 18:2-4)
13. to love the Lord your God with all your heart, to love your neighbor as yourself (Mark 12:28-31)
14. mother (John 21:26-27)
15. pleased (Luke 23:8)

---

When one team runs out of people, declare a winner and applaud everyone's efforts. Then ask:

● **What do you think about Jesus' life and teachings now that we've played this game?**

● **What do you think the gospel-writers wanted us to know about Jesus?**

● **How are the gospels like "good news" for the people of the world?**

● **How is the life of Jesus good news for you?**

Say: **This game gave us a quick introduction to a few**

important truths about Jesus' life. Now let's go a little deeper into the message of the gospels.

# ◆ Experience

Form four groups. Have each group find one story from one of the four gospels that group members think best represents who Jesus is. The story could describe any part of Jesus' life, from his birth to his death and resurrection.

Once groups have chosen their passages, have each group prepare to re-enact its passage. Allow several minutes for preparation, then have each group present its drama.

After each presentation, ask:

● **Why did you choose this passage to illustrate who Jesus is?**

● **What quality of Jesus does this story show?**

After all the presentations, ask:

● **How did it feel to present your dramas?**

● **How is presenting a drama about Jesus' life like trying to live like Jesus in real life? How is it different?**

● **How can we become more like Jesus in real life?**

Say: **The more we know about who Jesus is, the easier it is to trust him to control our lives. And as we give Christ control over what we do each day, we naturally begin to become more like him.**

# ◆ Grow

Give kids each a 3×5 card and a pencil, and say: **Jesus wants you to grow in your relationship with him. You can do that as you understand more about who he is. But to learn about him, you must be willing to read and study about him.**

**On your 3×5 card write "My Reading Schedule." Number the card from one to 30. Pick one of the four gospels to read. Decide how many chapters you'll need to read each day to complete the book in 30 days. Write the chapter numbers for each day on your card. Sign your card and ask another person to sign it as a witness. Agree to hold each other accountable in the coming weeks.**

**Go**

Say: **For our closing today, let's read how one of Jesus' disciples summed up who Jesus is.**

Ask a student to read aloud Matthew 16:13-16. As a closing prayer, tell students to repeat this prayer after you, one line at a time:

**Jesus, you are the Christ, the Son of the living God. Change our lives.**

**Jesus, you are the Christ, the Son of the living God. Change our group.**

**Jesus, you are the Christ, the Son of the living God. Change our world.**

**In Jesus' name, amen.**

# Why Two Testaments?

## ◆ Theme: Comparing the Old and New Testaments (Hebrews 1, 9)

Hebrews 1 and 9 vividly explain the culminating work of God in Christ. The author draws comparisons between the old covenant (testament) and God's glory in Christ (the new covenant). He portrays everything God had done in the Old Testament as preparation for the crowning glory of Jesus.

Kids will find these two chapters heavy in theological talk. Use this session to help them look beyond the language to see the wonderful message of redemption that unites the Old and New Testaments.

## ◆ Objectives

During this session kids will:
● compare the Old and New Testaments to yeast and bread;
● create a cartoon to explain Hebrews 1 and 9;
● experience being separated from God in the old covenant; and
● share the good news of Christ with a close friend or family member.

## ◆ Preparation

Read and study Hebrews 1 and 9.

Gather a bowl, yeast, sliced bread, Bibles, newsprint, markers, cookies or bowls of ice cream, a cross, paper and pencils.

# The Session

## ◆ Dig

Gather kids in a circle. Say: **This is going to be a tough, but exciting study. We're going to look at two chapters from the book of Hebrews that will help us understand why the Bible has a New and an Old Testament. Let's try an experiment to help you understand the truths we'll be exploring.**

Pass around a small bowl of yeast and ask kids to put some yeast in their palms. Then have them lick it out of their palms. Pass around a slice of bread and ask each person to tear off a small piece. Eat the bread together. Ask:

- **What's the difference between the yeast and the bread?**
- **Which would give you more nourishment?**

Say: **The reason we have the Old and New Testament is like the experience you just had with the yeast and bread. The Old Testament is like the yeast—it's a vital part of the bread, but by itself it can't do anything for us. The New Testament is like the bread. It completes the yeast (the Old Testament) to make something that can meet our needs so we can live.**

## ◆ Discover

Say: **Let's compare the Old and New Testaments more closely.**

Form four teams and assign each team one of these passages: Hebrews 1:1-4; 9:1-5; 9:6-10; and 9:11-15. Give groups each a sheet of newsprint and several markers. Have each group create a supersize cartoon strip that describes what happens in its passage.

Give students several minutes to create their cartoon strips. Be available to help kids with hard-to-picture items mentioned in the passages.

When kids are ready, have each group present its cartoon and explain what's happening in each panel. Then ask:

- **Did you enjoy this activity? Why or why not?**

- **What was hard about this activity?**
- **What did you discover from these passages?**
- **Why do you think the writer of Hebrews spent so much time comparing Old Testament things and New Testament things?**
- **What do you think is the most important thing to grasp in these passages?**

Ask someone to read Hebrews 9:15. Say: **There are many things in these passages that are hard to understand. But it all made perfect sense to the people of Jesus' day. And the point of it all is this: Jesus has done something to give each of us who believe in him an eternal inheritance. Through his death and resurrection we are set free from the chains of sin and the old covenant law.**

## ◆ Experience

Choose about one-fourth of your kids to be "high priests." Have the rest be "common people." Have the common people sit on the floor along the walls of the room. Gather the high priests in a circle in the center of the room, and give each a cookie or a bowl of ice cream. Listen patiently to the common people's complaints, but don't allow them to rise from the floor. Ask:

- **How does it feel to be a high priest? Explain.**
- **How does it feel to be a common person? Explain.**
- **How is this situation like the religious law in the Old Testament?**

Say: **In the Old Testament, only the high priests could enter the holy of holies, which housed the ark of the covenant. The rest of the people were forbidden to come before God's presence. But that wasn't the end of the story.**

Without saying anything else, hold up a cross and carry it to one of the common people. With cross in hand, help the common person to his or her feet and lead him or her to join the high priests. Repeat this procedure until all the common people are together with the high priests. As you serve the common people their snacks, ask:

- **How did you feel as I led you to join the high priests?**
- **Why do you think I carried a cross?**

**15**

● **How is what I did like what Jesus did for each of us through his death and resurrection?**

Say: **It's hard to comprehend what Christ has done. Through him we have a new covenant with God. We no longer have to rely on the high priest. Jesus is that priest. He opened the door for each of us to go directly to God. He also brought each of us salvation if we have faith in him and turn our lives over to him.**

## ◆ Grow

Give each student a piece of paper and a pencil. At the top of the paper, have them each write the name of their best friend or their closest family member. Then say: **We've talked a lot about how it used to be and also about the good news of the new covenant. For a moment think about who Jesus is in your life. Pretend your best friend or your closest family member has asked you to explain in writing exactly what the new covenant can do for him or her. What would you tell that person about Jesus, and the new covenant discussed in Hebrews 9?**

Give kids several minutes to write their letters. Kids may be hesitant at first, so be ready to suggest ways to start their letters or things they might include in them.

When the letters are completed, have volunteers read their letters to the rest of the group. Then have kids fold their letters and hold them in their laps.

## ◆ Go

Say: **The new covenant Jesus established in the New Testament is not supposed to be a secret. It was written to be shared with people everywhere. Let's celebrate the new covenant by sharing its truth with those people who are closest to us—our families and friends.**

Encourage kids to take a step of faith and deliver their letters to the people they wrote them to. Explain that it doesn't matter whether the people they wrote to are Christians, as long as kids' messages are clear and easy to understand.

Close with prayer, thanking God for the new covenant in Christ and for giving the message of Christ to share with others.

# I Wanna Be Like Jesus

## ◆ Theme: Being Like Jesus
(Matthew 10:7-40)

If you ask the average person what it means to be like Jesus, what would he or she tell you? Go to church? Be nice to your co-workers? Give to charity? All of these things are good, but when compared with the directives in Matthew 10, they present only a shallow portion of what it really means to be a disciple of Jesus.

This session helps kids tear away the veneer of "popular" Christianity to see the reality of what living like Jesus means. It's a discovery that's both sobering and exciting.

## ◆ Objectives
In this session kids will:
- hold a Jesus look-alike contest;
- discuss what it means to be like Jesus today;
- play a game to illustrate what it's like to follow Jesus; and
- give assignments to each other on how to be more like Jesus.

## ◆ Preparation
Read and study Matthew 10:7-40.

Gather yarn, scissors, tape, newsprint, Bibles, markers and pencils. You'll also need a copy of the "I Wanna Be Like Jesus" handout (page 22) for each person.

# The Session

## ◆ Dig

Form groups of six or fewer. Give each group yarn, scissors, tape and newsprint or old newspapers. Have groups each choose the person in their group they think looks most like Jesus. Then instruct groups to use their supplies to make their models look as much like Jesus as they possibly can.

Allow several minutes for kids to work. When the models are ready, have each "Jesus" present himself to the whole group. Applaud each group's efforts and award all the Jesus look-alikes first prize.

Say: **It's fun to try to look like Jesus on the outside, but today we're going to talk about what it would be like to live like Jesus on the inside. We're all called to be like Jesus, but that may involve more than you imagine. Let's find out.**

## ◆ Discover

Form four groups, and assign each group one of these passages: Matthew 10:7-10; 10:16-23; 10:24-31; and 10:32-40. Give each group a body-size sheet of newsprint and a marker. Have one person from each group lie on the newsprint while the other group members outline him or her on the newsprint. Say: **Study your passage. Then, in your Jesus outline, write how your passage applies to being like Jesus today.**

Let kids work for several minutes, but be ready to offer help if they have trouble understanding the meaning of a verse or can't see how it might apply to their lives.

When groups are ready, tape each of their Jesus outlines side-by-side on a wall. Review each group's responses, creating a composite of what it means to be like Jesus today. Then ask:

● **Does this composite surprise you? Why or why not?**

● **Do you think many people actually live like Jesus today? Why or why not?**

● If you lived according to this composite we've created, how would your life be different?

Say: **To live like Jesus today means much the same thing it meant back when Jesus was in human form on the earth. The instructions haven't changed. Before we see how we can take positive steps toward being more like Jesus, let's try to get a better understanding of what it's like to be a "radical" disciple like those described in Matthew 10.**

## ◆ Experience

Clear a large space in the meeting room. Form four groups: "disciples of Jesus," "persecutors," "demons" and "sick and dead people." Disperse the sick and dead people evenly around the room, then surround each of them with persecutors and demons. Line up the disciples of Jesus along one end of the room.

Say: **The object of the game is for the disciples of Jesus to touch the sick and dead people and say, "Jesus loves you" in order to heal them so they become disciples of Jesus too. But it's the job of the persecutors and demons to prevent the disciples of Jesus from reaching the sick and dead people.**

**Here are the rules of the game:**

**1. Sick and dead people may not move until they are "healed" by a disciple. Then they may get up and become disciples.**

**2. Demons may not touch the disciples of Jesus, but they may block their path to sick or dead people. The disciples of Jesus may not touch demons, but they may say, "I rebuke you" to get them to move out of their way.**

**3. Persecutors may block the disciples' path, and they may also grab the disciples by the wrist to prevent them from reaching the sick and dead people. Disciples may not touch the persecutors, but they may say, "I forgive you" to make the persecutors let go of their wrists and move out of their way.**

**4. Persecutors may grab disciples' wrists as often as they want. But when a persecutor is "forgiven" seven times, he or she becomes a disciple of Jesus.**

**5. Play continues until all the sick and dead people are healed.**

Start the game. When all the sick and dead people are healed, call a halt to the game and congratulate all the players on a fine performance.

## ◆ Grow

Call everyone together and ask:
● **What did you enjoy about this game? Explain.**
● **What was frustrating about this game? Explain.**
● **How did it feel to be a demon? a persecutor? a sick or dead person? a disciple of Jesus?**
● **How was this game similar to what it might be like to be like Jesus today?**
● **Who are the sick and dead people around us today?**
● **Who are the persecutors?**
● **How can disciples of Jesus heal others today?**
Say: **Being a disciple of Jesus, especially today, is an adventure full of challenges and obstacles. But Jesus has given us all the authority and grace we need to overcome evil and reach out to a hurting world with Christ's love.**

## ◆ Go

Read aloud Luke 4:18, then say: **This was Jesus' purpose when he was in human form on the earth, and it's also our purpose today. Let's close the meeting by challenging each other to be more like Jesus this week.**

Give kids each a copy of the "I Wanna Be Like Jesus" handout (page 22), tape and a pencil. Have kids tape their handouts to their backs. Then have kids walk around the room and give each other "assignments" corresponding to each of the sections of Luke 4:18. For example, for the first section, kids might write, "Tell one person this month about your faith in Jesus," or for the second section they might write, "Visit a prison and hand out Christian tracts with a group of friends."

Continue until all the kids have at least one assignment for each section on their handouts. Then say: **I challenge you to begin to live radically for Jesus this week by completing one of your assignments. Then complete another assignment each**

**week until they're all done. If you do this, it will change your life.**

Close with prayer, thanking God for showing kids what it means to be like Jesus today.

# I WANNA BE LIKE JESUS

## INSTRUCTIONS:

For each section of Luke 4:18 written below, create a corresponding "assignment" that will help you become more like Jesus.

- - - - - - - - - - - - - - - - - - - - - - - - - - - - - - - - - - - - - - - - ✂

## SECTION 1

The Spirit of the Lord is on me, because he has anointed me to preach good news to the poor.

## SECTION 2

He has sent me to proclaim freedom for the prisoners

## SECTION 3

and recovery of sight for the blind,

## SECTION 4

To release the oppressed

# Jesus, Parables and You

## ◆ Theme: Real-Life Lessons
(Matthew 13:10-17)

Jesus' words in Matthew 13:10-17 can seem perplexing for many readers. On the surface, he appears to say that he speaks in parables to confuse people. By digging deeper, however, we discover Jesus is explaining why some people fail to understand his messages.

Teenagers may wonder, as did the disciples, why Jesus answered people's questions with parables. In this session kids will discover what parables are, and how Jesus used them to reveal many of the deepest truths about himself and his kingdom.

## ◆ Objectives

During this session kids will:
● try to understand instructions from leaders who can't talk or write;
● explore why Jesus used parables;
● learn from each other through different methods; and
● make a commitment to read and study Jesus' parables.

## ◆ Preparation

Read and study Matthew 13:10-17.

Gather Bibles. Make one copy of the "Learning Methods" handout (page 27) and divide it into three sections as indicated.

---

# The Session

---

## ◆ Dig

Form groups of no more than four. Have the person in each group whose birthday is closest to the beginning of the school year be the leader for that group.

Gather the leaders and secretly give them these instructions: **Your job is to get the rest of your group to dance around the room while singing a song such as "Row, Row, Row Your Boat." But the trick is that you may not speak, write or mouth any words. You may only use facial expressions and hand signals. Go!**

After a few minutes, call time. If any groups were successful in this activity, congratulate them. Then ask:

● **How did you feel as you were trying to understand your leaders?**

● **How is this like the way people feel when they can't understand what someone is trying to tell them?**

● **How did you leaders feel when you were trying to tell the groups what to do?**

## ◆ Discover

Say: **Just as you may have felt frustrated in this first activity, Jesus' disciples felt frustrated, too, as he taught them in a different way than they were used to. Today we're going to explore why Jesus taught in parables.**

Have someone read aloud Matthew 13:10-17, then have two or three volunteers tell what they think the passage means.

Ask:

● **Is this an easy passage to understand? Why or why not?**

● **What's a parable?**

Say: **A parable is a story that has meaning on more than one level. For example, you might tell a story about a man who falls into a hole he dug by himself to illustrate how people fall into bad situations that they create for themselves in life.**

● **Did Jesus use parables so he could confuse the people he taught? Explain.**

● **From what you see in this passage, why do you think Jesus taught in parables?**

## ◆ Experience

Form three groups and give each a different portion of the "Learning Methods" handout (page 27). Say: **Read your group's handout and decide how you'll teach the message listed there, based on the handout's instructions.**

After a few minutes, have each small group present its "teaching time" for the rest of the group. After all three groups have taught their lessons, have kids vote on the teaching style that made the most sense to them.

## ◆ Grow

After the voting, ask:

● **How did you feel about each method used for teaching?**

● **Which teaching method did you learn the most from? Explain.**

● **Which method was most like the method Jesus used?**

● **Why was that method effective?**

Say: **Just as one of the groups used a familiar scene to tell about a bigger issue, Jesus used familiar stories to teach about heavenly issues. People who got stuck on the earthly meaning never really understood Jesus' true message.**

**Jesus' parables still challenge us today to think about our lives as Christians.**

**Go**

Say: **During the next few weeks, challenge yourself by
studying some of Jesus' parables in Matthew. For example,
examine the parables found in Matthew 13; 20; 21; and 22.
Try to figure out what they meant for the people during Jesus'
time and what they mean for you today.**

Form a circle. Have kids take turns saying one thing they appreciate about the way Jesus taught people. Then have volunteers
close in prayer, thanking God for challenging us through Jesus'
parables.

# LEARNING METHODS

## INSTRUCTIONS:

Photocopy and cut apart these sections, then give each section to a different group.

------------------------------------------------------------ ✂

## GROUP 1:

Your job is to teach the rest of the class that serving other people is important. You may do this only by reading the message listed below. You may not change any words in the message and must remain straight-faced during the teaching time.

"Serving people is important. We must all serve other people. It's really important to serve other people. We really mean it, serve other people because it's important to do so. You heard it here first: serve others."

------------------------------------------------------------

## GROUP 2:

Your job is to teach the rest of the group why it's important to help the poor. You may do this by telling the class members why it's important to help the poor. Using a monotonous voice, take turns explaining reasons for helping the poor. For example, you might say, "It's important to help the poor because they don't have much" or "It's good to help the poor because then you'll feel like you've done something for others."

------------------------------------------------------------

## GROUP 3:

Your job is to teach the rest of the group why it's important not to lie. You must come up with a story based on situations that really could happen that illustrate one or more reasons it's dangerous to lie. For example, you might tell a story about a student who stole an important test, then framed someone else for stealing it—causing that innocent person to flunk the class and miss out on an important scholarship to a big university. Have fun with your story, but don't lose sight of the message you're teaching.

# Walking on Water

## ◆ Theme: Faith (Matthew 14:22-33)

Peter was an excitable man. He charged in where other people hesitated. Sometimes his thoughtless zeal caused him to blunder, but other times it took him right into the center of God's will.

Teenagers often take steps of faith and then back down when their resolve weakens. They want to remain faithful to Christ, but they don't always know how to move beyond their fear. They become just like Peter on the water when he looked away from Jesus toward the storm and began to sink.

This session focuses on Peter's faith—and his fear. Through Peter's story, kids will discover the power of Jesus to conquer their fear and help them move on in faith.

## ◆ Objectives

During this session kids will:
- rank major fears in their lives;
- explore Peter's water-walking experience;
- experience the problems that come with taking their eyes off the target; and
- commit to working with Jesus to overcome fear with faith.

## ◆ Preparation

Read and study Matthew 14:22-33.
Gather paper, pencils, Bibles, a dart board and four darts.

# The Session

## ◆ Dig

Say: **Today we'll look at one of Peter's toughest experiences with Jesus. He did fine until his fear overcame his faith.**

**Fear is hard on all of us. Let's do an activity to discover the things we're most afraid of.**

Give each person a sheet of paper and a pencil. Have kids each list the 10 things they fear most in life. Their fears could be anything, but encourage them to make the fears as personal as possible. For example, a fear of being alone in life is more personal than a fear of nuclear war.

When kids have listed their fears, have them make two columns on the other sides of their papers. Have them title one column "Fears I can conquer," and the other, "Fears I can't conquer." Then have kids categorize their 10 fears into these two columns.

Have volunteers tell some of the fears they can conquer, then some of the fears they feel they can't conquer. Ask:

● **Do you think your fears are normal? Why or why not?**

● **Why do you think you could conquer some fears and not others?**

● **How is fear the opposite of faith?**

Say: **Fear is a normal part of life. It keeps us from jumping off cliffs and swimming toward sharks. But fear can become unhealthy when it keeps us from receiving the good things God has for us in life. Let's take a closer look at that kind of fear.**

## ◆ Discover

Say: **Peter had fears just like each of us. And sometimes his fears kept him from reaching Jesus. Let's relive Peter's experience with Jesus on the water.**

Gather kids into a boat shape on the floor. Hand out Bibles and designate one person as Peter.

Walk away from the group to the other side of the meeting

**29**

area. Ask kids to turn to Matthew 14:22-33.

Say: **We'll read this passage together, but I'll stop you at times and ask you to do different things.**

Have a volunteer read verses 22-24 aloud. Tell the group to sway like a boat tossed about by waves.

Have another volunteer read verses 25-26 aloud. Tell the group to shriek in fear as you walk toward them.

Say: **Take courage! It is I. Don't be afraid.**

Ask Peter to read aloud verse 28. Then have Peter get out of the boat and walk slowly toward you.

Have the boat people read verse 30 loudly.

Reach out your hand and lead Peter back to the safety of the boat.

Have the whole group read verses 32-33 in unison.

After the experience, call everyone together and ask:

● **What do you think about Peter's decision to get into the water?**

● **What would you have done if you had been Peter?**

● **What do you think got Peter in trouble?**

● **What did Peter need to do to escape his fear?**

Say: **When you're afraid, it's easy to take your eyes off Christ. You're thinking about everything happening to you, and you lose sight of the truth that Jesus can help you.**

## ◆ Experience

Say: **Let's see how Peter's experience with Jesus applies to us. But let's have some fun with it.**

Set up a dart board at one end of the room. About 8 feet away from the board, gather kids in a huddle around you. Hold up four darts and say: **Each of you is going to throw these four darts at the dart board. You'll throw the first two while looking at the board, but you'll throw the last two while looking at the ceiling or way off to the side.**

Line kids up and have them each throw the darts. Have fun laughing at kids' poor shots and praising kids' efforts when they're looking at the target.

# ◆ Grow

After everyone has thrown the darts, ask:

● **How did it feel to throw darts without being able to take careful aim?**

● **How did your marksmanship change when you looked away?**

● **How is throwing these darts without looking like trying to overcome our fears without Jesus' help?**

● **What happens when we try to be courageous on our own?**

● **How can we overcome our fears?**

Say: **Fear is a feeling, but faith is an act of will. Even when we're afraid, we can choose to keep our eyes on Jesus and trust him to see us through rough times. As long as we trust him, our fears will not overcome us.**

# ◆ Go

Say: **Unlike Peter, we don't have to let the storm that rages around us take our eyes off Jesus. We can choose to trust him, no matter what our circumstances. Let's close today by demonstrating our faith through Peter's story.**

Have kids gather back into their boat shape. Read aloud Matthew 14:22-33, and have kids follow the motions of the passage as before. Only this time, have everyone step out into the "water" when Peter does. With all the kids in the water, form a circle, hold hands and thank God that kids can trust him no matter how often fear tries to make them turn away.

# God Is Not Fair!

## ◆ Theme: Fairness (Matthew 20:1-16)

If God is fair, why are some people born rich or intelligent, while others are born poor or mentally handicapped? If God is fair, why are some people talented or beautiful while others are ordinary or plain?

The answer is simple, as pointed out in Matthew 20:1-16—God is not fair by our standards of fairness. He does not give everyone equal abilities or equal chances to succeed on earth. But God *is* just. No matter what circumstance we find ourselves in, God's grace will always be sufficient to enable us to overcome it.

It isn't easy to draw the fine line between what's fair and what's just. This session helps kids understand the nature of God's heart when it comes to fairness and justice.

## ◆ Objectives

In this session kids will:
- tell their most embarrassing moments;
- rewrite Matthew 20:1-16 using three different scenarios;
- perform tasks of varying difficulty for the same pay; and
- discuss the difference between being fair and being just.

## ◆ Preparation

Read and study Matthew 20:1-16.

Gather paper, Bibles, pencils and 3×5 cards. You'll also need a quarter to give to each person.

# The Session

## ◆ Dig

Have kids form a circle, and ask each person to share his or her most embarrassing moment. If your group is large, form several smaller groups so all the kids can share.

After everyone has shared, say: **News flash! The government has just declared that anyone having an embarrassing moment is worthy of death! All of you are hereby convicted of embarrassment and sentenced to die at the hands of an assassin!**

Have kids line up shoulder to shoulder, and choose one person from the group to be the assassin. Give the assassin three paper wads (call them grenades) and have him or her stand in front of the group. Then say: **Although you are all worthy of death, unfortunately we have only three grenades in our church armory today. So only three of you will die. The rest will be set free.**

Have the assassin throw a paper wad at three different people. Have those three people feign death.

After all the paper wads are thrown, call everyone together and ask:

● **Is it fair that, although all of you were condemned to die, only three of you actually paid the price? Why or why not?**

● **Is it just that the three who were condemned did, in fact, die for their crimes?**

● **What's the difference between justice and fairness?**

Say: **Most people think justice and fairness are interchangeable words. But in truth they mean different things. Fairness means that everyone is treated exactly the same. Justice means that each person gets all that he or she needs or deserves. To understand the difference better, let's look at a passage of scripture where Jesus talks about justice and fairness.**

## ◆ Discover

Form three groups and have them read Matthew 20:1-16. Give them pencils and paper. Assign each group one of the following

**33**

settings and have them rewrite Jesus' parable as though it had happened in that setting.

- at school
- at home with brothers and sisters
- at a church fund-raiser

When groups are ready, have them read aloud their rewritten parables. Then ask:

- **Do these situations seem fair to you? Why or why not?**

Say: **Jesus' idea of justice may go against popular opinion today, just as it did back in the first century. But before we find out why God sees justice in this way, let's do a little exercise to help us understand what it feels like to be on the receiving end of justice.**

## ◆ Experience

Have kids form a circle. Assign each person one of the tasks below, and tell them all that they'll receive a prize when they complete their tasks. (It's okay if more than one person gets the same task.)

- Stand on your head and sing "My Country 'Tis of Thee."
- Sit quietly.
- Multiply $1,002 \times 34 \times 568.43 \times 349,093.0001 \times .0005$ by hand.
- Run 25 laps around the room.
- Take off your shoes and relax.
- Do 25 push-ups.
- Pick up all the trash in the room.

You may add other assignments if you wish. When all the kids have completed their tasks, call them together and award each person a quarter.

## ◆ Grow

Ask:

- **How did you feel when you saw I gave some people easy tasks and other people difficult tasks? Explain.**
- **How did you feel when I paid you all the same amount for doing different tasks? Explain.**

● **How is this like Jesus' definition of justice?**

Say: **Each of you performed a task for a prize. I didn't tell you what your prize was, nor did I say you'd get a bigger prize for doing a harder task. You each got what you agreed to.**

**According to God's definition of justice, the pay is the same for all Christians—eternal life with Jesus.**

Ask:

● **With what you know now about God's ways, do you think God is fair?**

● **Was it fair for Jesus to die on the cross for our sins?**

● **Was it just for him to die?**

Say: **God is not fair by our definition of fairness. If he were, Jesus would never have gone to the cross, since he never did anything wrong. But God is just.**

 **Go**

Give each student a pencil and a 3×5 card. Say: **On your card write three areas of your life that you feel are unfair. Then on the back of the card, write a just reason God might have for allowing each of these things in your life. For example, you might like someone who doesn't like you in return. That seems unfair. But in his justice, God might allow this unfairness to help you learn to love unconditionally—like Jesus does.**

When kids are finished, have volunteers share what they wrote, then say: **God's ways are sometimes hard to understand. But we can be assured that God will treat each of us with love and justice all the time.**

Close with prayer, thanking God for his justice and asking him to strengthen kids to face the unfair situations they face in life.

# The Winning Combination

## ◆ Theme: Sharing Faith (Mark 4:3-20)

When Christians share their faith, they may be surprised at the range of reactions they get. Like the different seeds in the parable of the sower, different people react differently. Some people are all ears, thankful for the opportunity to hear of God's love for them. Others react to the same message with boredom—or even anger.

This session will help kids realize that the results of a witnessing encounter don't rest in their hands. God wants all of us to share our faith with friends, even though some friends may be more ready to hear than others.

## ◆ Objectives:

During this session kids will:
- explore Mark 4:3-20;
- consider why some people respond to Jesus' message and others don't;
- develop their own personal statements of faith to share with friends; and
- pray for friends who seem ready to make faith commitments to Christ.

## ◆ Preparation

Read and study Mark 4:3-20.

Gather a child's jigsaw puzzle, Bibles, pencils, paper and 3×5 cards. Make a copy of the "Soil Search" handout (page 40) for each person.

Set up a "wall" by hanging a sheet from the ceiling. Place a chair on each side of the screen.

# The Session

##  Dig

Hand each person one piece of a child's jigsaw puzzle. Make sure each piece has a "mate" somewhere else in the room. Tell kids to quickly find the right combination—a puzzle piece that fits with theirs. The first pair of kids to find a fit wins.

When everyone has found a fit, congratulate kids on their efforts. Then ask:

● **What was fun about this activity?**

● **What are some other things in life, besides puzzles, that need the right combinations to work?**

● **What about gardening? How does that activity require the right combination?**

Say: **Today we're going to think about what it means to share our faith with our friends. In the Bible, Jesus used a gardening story—the parable of the sower—to illustrate how ready the "soil" of some people's hearts may be to hear about God and respond with a lifelong commitment.**

## ◆ Discover

Say: **Let's look at this parable more closely.**

Have kids turn to the parable of the sower in Mark 4:3-20. Ask a volunteer to read the parable aloud, then distribute the "Soil Search" handout (page 40) and pencils. Have kids work silently for a few minutes, then ask volunteers to tell what they wrote. Ask:

● **What does this parable tell us about how easy or hard it is to lead someone to a faith commitment to Jesus?**

● **How does this parable affect the way you view sharing your faith with others? Explain.**

Say: **We can't make anyone choose to follow Christ, any more than we can make a plant produce fruit. But we can help create the right conditions for God to draw a person to him, and we can help a person move toward Christ when he or she is ready to make a faith commitment.**

## ◆ Experience

Form pairs and have each pair decide which partner will play the role of a farmer and which will be the soil. Tell the farmers each to prepare a message that they think would encourage their partners. The message must be either a scripture verse, an encouraging word or a handshake. The message will be conveyed by each farmer as he or she sits on the opposite side of the sheet "wall" from his or her partner.

Tell the farmers that they must decide whether to:

● convey the message in writing,

● whisper it through the sheet or

● reach under the sheet to offer a handshake.

Without informing the farmers of their choices, have the soils each choose to either close their eyes, plug their ears or hold their hands "tied" behind their backs.

When pairs are ready, have them take turns trying to communicate and receive the encouraging message. The winners are those pairs that successfully gave and received the "word"; that is, they found the right combination of message-sending and receiver-readiness.

After you declare the winners, ask:

● **How did it feel to deliver your message of encouragement?**

● **How did it feel to receive the message?**

● **How did it feel not to receive the message?**

● **How is this like sharing your faith with your friends?**

● **What makes a person ready to hear the gospel message?**

● **What do you need to do to be ready to share the message of Christ with others?**

# ◆ Grow

Say: **We've thought a lot about what kinds of soil we'll find in people we speak to about our faith. But we'll never be able to tell others what Christ means to us if we don't know what to say. Let's see if we can solve that problem right now.**

Give kids paper and pencils and have them write personal statements describing how Jesus has changed their lives. Encourage kids to be as realistic as possible about what they might actually say to a friend. For kids who have trouble, help them by asking questions such as, "How has Jesus affected your priorities? your friendships? your free time?"

After a few minutes, have kids find their original partners. Ask pairs to role play sharing their personal statements in front of the whole group. Applaud kids' courage and honesty.

Say: **Sharing your faith doesn't mean reciting a bunch of theological jargon. It simply means sharing what Jesus means to you and how he has changed your life. And, as we now can see, all of us can do that.**

# ◆ Go

Distribute 3×5 cards and ask kids each to jot down the name of one friend who seems to be "good soil"—ready to learn more about Christ's message. Ask kids to silently pray for an opportunity to tell these people about their faith during the next month.

After a few moments of silence, close with prayer, thanking God for giving kids new life in Christ and for calling them to share that life with the people around them.

# SOIL SEARCH

Mark 4:3-20

## INSTRUCTIONS:

Study the parable, then fill in the blanks and answer the questions related to each kind of soil Jesus describes.

1. First type of soil: The seed falls on the _____.
What does Satan do to the Word?


What might be a real-life example of this today?


2. Second type of soil: The seed falls on the _____.
What happens to the Word?


What might be a real-life example of this today?


3. Third type of soil: The seed falls in the _____.
What do worries and desires do to the Word?


How might this happen in teenagers' lives today?


4. Fourth type of soil: The seed falls on _____.
What does the Word do when it hits this soil?


What might be a real-life example of this today?

# Dollars and Sense

## ◆ Theme: True Wealth (Mark 10:17-27)

Mark 10:17-27 tells the story of a rich young man who wants to get into heaven. But he turns away from following Jesus because he loves his wealth more than God. The story ends with Jesus making an alarming statement—that it's easier for a camel to go through the eye of a needle than for a rich man to enter heaven.

Teenagers know all too well about money... and how it can run people's lives. As kids begin to earn money, they discover a "wealth" of options for their ever-growing independence. Use this session to help them decide whether to use their money to pursue the world's version of the good life, or to submit their income to Jesus and seek heavenly riches by serving him.

## ◆ Objectives

During this session participants will:
● brainstorm ways to become wealthy;
● examine Jesus' lesson of the rich young man;
● experience how it feels to try to convince someone how good their own work is; and
● encourage each other to seek heavenly riches.

## ◆ Preparation

Read and study Mark 10:17-27.

You'll need paper, pencils, a needle, a stuffed animal, Bibles and play money.

Make a copy of the "Money for Somethin' " handout (page 45) for each person.

# The Session

## ◆ Dig

Form groups of no more than four. Give each group a sheet of paper and a pencil. Say: **Each group has five minutes to brainstorm how to become the wealthiest group of people in the world. Write your methods for making money on your papers. Go!**

After five minutes call time. Have groups tell their ideas and how much money they think they'd earn.

Ask:

- **Did you like this activity? Why or why not?**
- **How is that like the way people often feel about money?**
- **Why do people wish they could be millionaires?**
- **Do you want to be wealthy? Why or why not?**

## ◆ Discover

Say: **Being wealthy is probably a goal we all have had at one time or another. But wealth brings many potential problems to our lives and even to our faith.**

Give a volunteer a needle. Then hand him or her a stuffed animal. Say: **You have 10 seconds to get the animal through the eye of the needle. If you can't do it, pass the needle and the animal to the person next to you so he or she can try. Continue until I stop you or someone succeeds. Go.**

After everyone has tried, call time and ask:

- **How did you feel as you tried to do this activity?**

Have a volunteer read aloud Mark 10:17-27. Ask:

- **What do you think the main point of this scripture passage is?**
- **How is the way you felt with the needle and the stuffed animal like the way the rich man might've felt after hearing Jesus speak?**
- **Does this passage imply that wealth is bad? Why or why not?**

**42**

● **Why is Jesus worried about wealthy people?**

# ◆ Experience

Give each person a copy of the "Money for Somethin' " hand-out (page 45) and a pencil. Say: **Complete your handout, then find someone whose score is similar to yours and form a pair.**

When pairs are formed, say: **Now convince your partner that your score is better than his or hers. You have two minutes to do this.**

When time is up, have volunteers tell why their scores are best. Encourage kids to challenge what their partners say.

After a few minutes, have kids form a circle and tell if they liked this activity.

# ◆ Grow

Ask:

● **How did you feel as you tried to convince your partner your score was better?**

● **How is that like the way people act when they want to be wealthy?**

● **What bad attitudes can come from wanting to have lots of money?**

● **How do those attitudes go against what Jesus teaches about what's important?**

● **How can you apply what you've learned from this activity to your own lifestyle?**

# ◆ Go

Form groups of no more than four. Give kids each a pencil and one play money bill for each of the other people in their group. Say: **Jesus told the story of the rich man to warn us that money can take the place of God and keep us from serving him freely. Instead of earthly riches, we're to seek heavenly riches by loving and serving others. On each of your play money bills, write the name of a different person in your group. Then write one way that person can seek heavenly riches instead of earthly riches.**

**43**

After kids are done writing, have them give their play money to the appropriate group members. Then have small groups close in prayer, thanking God for this lesson from Mark and the warning it has for them.

Encourage kids to keep their play money in their wallets or purses as reminders not to let money become too important in their lives.

# MONEY FOR SOMETHIN'

## INSTRUCTIONS:
Respond to the following questions with a rating from 1 to 10, with 1 meaning, "This has little value to me," and 10 meaning, "I can't live without this." Then total your score and write it at the bottom of the page.

How valuable is . . .

. . . a $1,000 shopping spree at your favorite clothing store?

1    2    3    4    5    6    7    8    9    10

. . . a new sports car of your choice?

1    2    3    4    5    6    7    8    9    10

. . . a lifetime of free meals at the fast-food restaurant of your choice?

1    2    3    4    5    6    7    8    9    10

. . . 500 movie tickets to any theaters in the country?

1    2    3    4    5    6    7    8    9    10

. . . the best home-entertainment system money can buy?

1    2    3    4    5    6    7    8    9    10

. . . a two-month vacation to a tropical paradise?

1    2    3    4    5    6    7    8    9    10

. . . free jewelry and watches from any expensive jewelry store?

1    2    3    4    5    6    7    8    9    10

. . . limousine service to school every day until you graduate from college?

1    2    3    4    5    6    7    8    9    10

. . . a full-time maid to clean up your room and a chef to cook all your meals?

1    2    3    4    5    6    7    8    9    10

Final score:_____

# Don't Worry, Be His

### ◆ Theme: Priorities (Luke 12:22-34)

Jesus' words in this passage encourage us to totally trust in God, putting him first in everything. Allowing our heavenly Father to take care of us in this way frees us from the worries that many people dwell on.

Kids today have lots of pressures and worries. They also have lots of bad examples—from the media, the world of sports and even the church—for setting priorities. This session will help kids see the importance of setting their sights on God and allowing him to put the other things in their lives in their proper places.

### ◆ Objectives

During this session kids will:
● compare their priorities;
● examine Jesus' teaching on seeking God's kingdom;
● experience finding a big prize or little prizes; and
● commit with a partner to seeking God's kingdom in specific ways.

### ◆ Preparation

Read and study Luke 12:22-34.

Hide small prizes such as sticks of gum or small pieces of candy around the room in obvious and not-so-obvious places. Hide one big prize, such as a box of chocolates, in a very hard-to-find place. On the big prize write, "Big Prize."

Gather three balloons for each person, markers, straight pins, old magazines, Bibles and newsprint or a chalkboard. Make a copy of the "Seekers' Success" handout (page 50) for each person.

# The Session

## ◆ Dig

Give each student three balloons to inflate and tie off. Tell kids each to think of the three things they believe are most important to do or to have in life. Have kids use markers to secretly write each thing on a separate balloon.

Give each person a straight pin. Say: **When I say "go," bat your first balloon in the air. As a balloon comes to you, if what's written on it is the same as something you've written on one of your balloons, bat it back toward someone else. If what's written on it is different, pop it with your pin. After you pop a balloon, bat another of yours into the air. Try to keep all the unpopped balloons in the air. Keep going until you've stopped popping balloons.**

When kids have gone about 30 seconds without popping a balloon, stop the game and gather any remaining balloons.

Ask:

● **Did you all think the same things are important?**

● **How many priorities did you agree on? Why are they important?**

Say: **Different things are important to different people. But as Christians, there are certain things we can all agree on. Today we're going to be looking at what Jesus said is important for us.**

## ◆ Discover

Form two teams and distribute old magazines. Slowly read aloud Luke 12:22-34. Pause after each item mentioned in the pas-

**47**

sage for kids to find and rip out a picture of that item in their magazines. For example, the first item mentioned in the NIV is "what you will eat." Give 1 point to the first team to hold up a picture of a food item. You might need to be lenient on some items, allowing any picture of flowers to represent "lilies," for example.

After the first item has been found, go on to the next item. Continue through the entire passage, keeping score and having teams keep their pictures in piles.

When you've finished the passage, ask:

● **How would you like to have unlimited access to all the things in the pictures you've ripped out? Explain.**

● **What does the passage we just read have to say about those things?**

● **What does it mean to seek God's kingdom?**

## ◆ Experience

Form two teams. Give each person on one team the first set of instructions from the "Seekers' Success" handout (page 50). Give each person on the other team the other set of instructions. Don't let teams know that their instructions are different. Let teams begin seeking the prize, following the instructions they've been given.

When someone finds the "Big Prize," have the person who found it read the instructions he or she was following. Then have someone with different instructions read them.

Ask:

● **What helped you find the prize?**

● **Did the team that was told to have fun really have more fun than the other team? Why or why not?**

● **How did you feel when you found the prize?**

● **How are these two teams' methods like the ways different people seek God's kingdom today?**

● **What does God do for people who put him first?**

## ◆ Grow

Say: **Some people spend all their time and energy seeking pleasure. But in doing that, they often miss out on the most important things. Let's look again at Luke 12:29-31 to remem-**

ber what Jesus says is most important.

Have someone read the passage aloud while everyone follows along. Ask:

● **What things can Christian teenagers do to show that they are seeking God's kingdom above all else?**

Have kids brainstorm a list of actions. Write their responses on a chalkboard or newsprint.

 **Go**

Form pairs. Ask pairs to look over the list and choose one action they want to work on together, then indicate their commitment by initialing the action they've chosen. Have partners work together to plan ways they'll make changes in their lives and exchange phone numbers so they can call each other throughout the coming week to check on how their plans are working.

Close with prayer, asking God to help kids follow through on their commitments to seek him first.

# SEEKERS' SUCCESS

## INSTRUCTIONS:
Photocopy and cut apart the following instructions for each team.

------------------------------------------------------------- ✄

### Team Instructions

There's a big prize to be found somewhere nearby. Look for it in obvious places. Don't look anywhere that's difficult. Have fun while you're looking. If you don't find it, enjoy what you find along the way. Don't wear yourselves out searching—take a break whenever you want. If you think you've found the big prize, ask the leader.

-------------------------------------------------------------

### Team Instructions

There's a big prize to be found somewhere nearby. Look everywhere to find it. If you find other little things along the way, ignore them. You'll know it when you find the real prize. Don't let anyone distract you from your task. Keep at it until you succeed.

-------------------------------------------------------------

# I Did It My Way

## ◆ Theme: God's Love (Luke 15:11-24)

The story we know as "The Prodigal Son" could more accurately be called "The Loving Father." The real point of the story isn't what the son did, but how the father responded to the son's actions.

Many kids today don't know a good father's love. So be careful in this session not to relate God's love to any human father's love. The father in Luke 15 is a good example to keep before the kids.

As you work through this session, you'll be able to help kids see how much God loves them and encourage them to seek forgiveness so they can live their lives in the love God offers.

## ◆ Objectives

During this session kids will:
● think about why God loves them;
● prepare a creative presentation of Luke 15:11-24;
● feel how hard it is to forgive; and
● thank God for the gift of forgiveness in their own lives.

## ◆ Preparation

Read and study Luke 15:11-24.

Bring a roll of nickels and three bowls to your session. Before the session, secretly instruct one person to gather up all the nickels and insist on keeping them when his or her turn comes up in the Experience section.

Gather a chalkboard and chalk or newsprint and markers, Bibles, pencils and 3×5 cards.

# The Session

## ◆ Dig

As kids arrive, write on a chalkboard or newsprint the phrase, "I think God loves me because ..." Offer the chalk or marker to kids and have them each come up and write at least one completion of that phrase.

When everyone has written at least one completion, ask:

● **Looking at all the things we've written, what do you think are the most important ways we know God loves us?**

Say: **One way we know God loves us is the way he forgives us when we hurt him. We're going to be taking a look at God's love and forgiveness today.**

## ◆ Discover

Form groups of three and have each group come up with a present-day version of the story in Luke 15:11-24 to act out for the rest of the group. For a fun twist, have kids play the characters as animals rather than people. For example, a group could have the characters be a family of elephants or penguins.

When kids have finished presenting the scripture passage, ask:

● **Why did the father give the son his inheritance?**

● **Why did the father forgive the son after he'd blown the money?**

● **Why do you think Jesus told this story?**

● **Why does God love us the way the father loved the son in this story?**

## ◆ Experience

Empty a roll of nickels into a bowl at one end of the room. Form two teams and have them line up at the other end of the room. Place an empty bowl on the floor in front of each team. Tell kids that the object of the game is to get as many nickels in their bowls as they can. The first person on each team must run to the bowl of

**52**

nickels, place a nickel on his or her nose, walk carefully back and deposit the nickel in his or her team's bowl. Then the next person on the team must race for a nickel. If a nickel is dropped, it must go back into the first bowl, and the next person on the team must attempt the next nickel.

When your previously arranged nickel-stealer takes the nickels, respond in surprise. But then just say: Well, I guess that ends our game.

Have kids return to their seats, then ask:

● **What happened in our game?**

● **Did the nickel-stealer treat everyone fairly?**

● **How do you feel toward the person who took all the nickels?**

● **Based on the way God treats us, how should we act toward the person who took all the nickels?**

After your discussion, tell kids about the setup and get your nickels back.

Say: **It wasn't easy to think about forgiving the person who'd taken all the nickels. But God forgives us for far more than stealing a few nickels.**

## ◆ Grow

Draw two columns on a chalkboard or newsprint. At the top of one column write "Lovable," and at the top of the other write "Tough to Love." Have kids brainstorm qualities typical of teenagers that would make it easy or hard for God to love them.

When you've written at least six things in the "Tough to Love" category, ask:

● **If you were God looking at these lists, would you love us?**

Have several kids respond and explain their answers, then give your own response.

Say: **As tough as we are to love sometimes, God loves us anyway—no matter what we do. He may not like things we do, but those things don't make him love us any less. And God is always ready to forgive us and restore our relationship if we return to him—just like the father did in our scripture passage.**

**Go**

Be sensitive to your kids' feelings. It might be an appropriate time to challenge them to make a faith commitment or renew a commitment they've already made.

Have someone read aloud 1 John 1:8-9. Give kids each a pencil and a 3×5 card. Have kids write on their cards the sins that separate them from God, as the son in the scripture was separated from his father. Be sure kids know that no one will read what they write. When all kids have finished, have a time of silent prayer, encouraging kids to ask God's forgiveness. Close the prayer time with your own prayer of repentance.

When your prayer time is finished, have kids tear their 3×5 cards into tiny pieces. Together, throw the pieces in the air and shout, "Thanks, God, for forgiving me!"

# Servanthood Means Action

## ◆ Theme: True Servanthood
### (Luke 19:11-27; Matthew 20:26-27)

Jesus' parable of the talents in Luke 19:11-27 is often used to encourage people to invest their abilities for God. But there's another lesson found here, waiting just beneath the surface. The three workers in the parable were servants of the master. As Christians, we, too, are servants of our Master. By digging a little deeper into this passage, we can learn one vital quality that Jesus required of his servants—action!

Matthew 20:26-27 further supports this truth by reminding us that, to Jesus, the greatest person in the kingdom is the one who actively serves others.

Teenagers are often accused of trying to get away with doing as little as possible to help others. But this passage suggests we should go above and beyond what's expected by those around us, especially when it comes to serving God and meeting others' needs.

## ◆ Objectives

During this session kids will:
- learn what it's like to serve others;
- discover how it feels to be served;
- explore Jesus' teaching about servanthood in action; and
- commit to doing one act of service during the coming week.

## ◆ Preparation

Read and study Luke 19:11-27 and Matthew 20:26-27.

You'll need frosting, paper towels, plain cookies, a Bible, bowls, water and cloth towels.

# The Session

## ◆ Dig

Form three teams and have a different color of frosting prepared for each one. (If your group is larger than 15, form teams of no more than six.)

Place paper towels on a table and have teams sit around the table. Place a supply of cookies and a bowl of different-color frosting in front of each team.

Say: **On "go," you'll have three minutes to frost as many cookies as you can with your team's frosting. You may simply frost your own team's cookies or try to cover other teams' cookies as well. The team with its frosting color on the most cookies when time is up wins.**

**Oh yes, you may not use any utensils to frost the cookies— you must use your hands.**

Have kids wash their hands before starting the game and remind them not to lick their fingers. After three minutes, call time and declare a winner. Tell kids not to wash their hands.

## ◆ Discover

Read aloud Luke 19:11-27. Then ask:

● **What does this passage mean in relation to serving God?**

● **How is trying to frost the most cookies like trying to make the most out of what you've been given?**

● **In frosting the cookies I gave you, how were you like or unlike the servants in this parable?**

● **How can we take what God has given us and make those gifts more valuable?**

Open your Bible to Matthew 20:26-27, then hold it so a volunteer can read the passage. Ask:

● **What does Jesus tell us in this passage about serving?**

● **How is the way I helped the reader by holding the Bible an act of servanthood?**

56

Say: **In these passages, Jesus teaches that we are to go above and beyond what's expected in serving God and others. And sometimes that may be uncomfortable for us.**

# ◆ Experience

Form groups of three or four. Give each group a bowl of water and a towel and have group members form a circle around the water. Place a water-filled bowl and a towel next to you also, and call up one person from each group. Without saying a word, wash the frosting off the hands of each group's representative. Be very gentle and try to make as much eye contact as possible.

When you're finished, send the representatives back to their groups. Say to those whose hands you washed: **Now wash the frosting off the hands of the person on your right. Then have that person wash the hands of the person to his or her right. Continue until all members of your group have had their hands washed. Be gentle, thorough and considerate in your hand-washing.**

Walk around and observe how people wash each other's hands.

# ◆ Grow

After the hand-washing experience, comment on what you observed. Then ask:

● **How did you feel as someone washed your hands?**

● **How did you feel as you washed someone else's hands?**

● **How is that like the way it feels to be a servant?**

● **How did people in your group "go the extra mile" in the hand-washing experience?**

● **In what ways has Jesus "washed your hands" in the past?**

● **Is it easy to serve others above and beyond what's expected? Explain.**

# ◆ Go

Form pairs. Instruct partners to work together to come up with a servant project they'll do together in the coming week. It could be anything from raking leaves in a neighbor's yard to inviting a

**57**

lonely classmate over to spend time with them. Give pairs a few minutes to discuss their projects, then have volunteers share what they will do.

Have partners exchange phone numbers and encourage pairs to call you as well to let you know how their servant project went.

Have partners close in prayer, thanking God for showing them the true nature of servanthood in his son, Jesus.

After the prayer, have kids enjoy their frosted cookies.

# Give Me a Drink!

## ◆ Theme: Living Water (John 4:1-14)

Without ordinary water, life on Earth would be impossible. And in John 4, Jesus points out that without his "living" water, eternal life is impossible. We must "drink" from Christ's life for that life to spring up within us.

This session compares the qualities of ordinary water to the qualities of the living water Jesus described to the woman at the well. Use this session to help kids understand how they can drink the living water Christ offers.

## ◆ Objectives

In this session kids will:
- name the benefits of water;
- act out Jesus' encounter with the woman at the well;
- participate in a relay race to save their "lives"; and
- discover how God's living water can flow through them.

## ◆ Preparation

Read and study John 4:1-14.

This session works best in an outdoor setting, such as your church parking lot or a nearby basketball court. You'll need round balloons, Bibles, water guns for each person, access to a faucet, one Ping-Pong ball for every three people and fine-point permanent markers.

# The Session

## ◆ Dig

Fill a round balloon half-full with water and fill the other half with air. Gather kids in a circle. In "hot potato" fashion, toss the balloon around the circle. As each person catches the balloon, have him or her name one benefit of water before passing the balloon to someone else. Have an extra balloon on hand in case the first one accidentally breaks.

Count kids "out" if they hold the balloon for more than five seconds, or if they pass it without naming a benefit of water that hasn't already been named. Continue until only one person remains.

After the game, hold up the balloon and say: **It's clear that water has even more benefits than we can name here. But for all the good things this water represents, there is a water that's even better than this. Today we're going to find out more about this "better" water.**

## ◆ Discover

Form two groups and give each person a Bible. Have groups read John 4:1-14. Ask one group to prepare to re-enact the passage. Have group members assign parts for Jesus and the woman. Also assign kids to be the props, such as the well and the water.

Have the other group be the "special effects" group. While the first group is performing, have this group make special sounds to add to the action whenever they hear certain words. Here's a list of the key words and the effects that go with them:

- "water"—Gush! Gush! Gush!
- "life" or "living"—It's alive! It's alive!
- "drink(s)"—Gurgle, gurgle, gurgle!
- "thirst(y)"—Water! Water!

Practice the sound effects until the special effects group knows them. When kids are ready, have the first group enact the passage while the other group adds its special effects at the appropriate times.

**60**

After the performance, call everyone together and say: **Acting out this scripture passage was fun, wasn't it? But even in the fun, we can see that the passage is talking about something very serious—God's living water.**

Ask:

● **What difference does Jesus say there is between regular water and his living water?**

● **Do you think the woman really understood what he meant by "living" water? Explain.**

● **What do you think Jesus meant?**

Say: **Jesus was referring to himself as the living water. When we allow him to live through us, a wellspring of refreshing life flows out of us continuously.**

# ◆ Experience

Say: **Now that we understand what living water is, let's try to understand how this water can affect our lives.**

Find a large clear area in your church parking lot or use a nearby outdoor basketball court. Distribute small water guns and have kids fill them at an outdoor faucet.

When all the guns are filled, form teams of three and give each team a Ping-Pong ball. Set up a starting line and a finish line on the parking lot or basketball court.

Hold up a Ping-Pong ball and say: **Your Ping-Pong ball represents your life—your private needs and desires, as well as your relationships. Your team's goal is to save your life by moving it from the start line to the finish line over there. But, you can only move the ball by squirting it with your water gun.**

Place one member of each team at the starting line with a Ping-Pong ball and space the other two team members at one-third and two-third intervals along the course. Explain to starting team members that on "go," they are to shoot their Ping-Pong balls to their teammates, who will then shoot them to the next teammates, who will then shoot them across the finish line.

Start the relay. Allow all the teams to finish before congratulating the winning team. Collect the Ping-Pong balls and have kids form a circle and set their water guns on the ground in front of them.

# ◆ Grow

Ask:

● How did you feel as you tried to shoot the ball with your water gun?

● How was the ball being guided toward the finish line by water like letting God's living water flow through you in your daily life?

● How is running this race as a relay like the relationships we have with each other as fellow carriers of God's living water?

● What are some ways Christ's living water in you can bring life to you—or the people around you?

● How do we get Christ's living water?

Say: **According to John 4, to get Christ's living water, all we have to do is ask for it and choose to live our lives in obedience to Christ. Once we do that, Jesus says his living water will spring up within us.**

# ◆ Go

Give each person a fine-point permanent marker and a Ping-Pong ball. On their Ping-Pong balls, have kids write "John 4:14." Say: **Take these balls home as a reminder to always ask God to give you his living water, so you can become a spring of life to the world around you.**

Close with prayer, asking God to give kids his living water and to become within them a spring of eternal life.

# You Can Be Too Careful!

## ◆ Theme: Trust (John 20:24-31)

Doubting is easy. And it's often necessary in today's world. If we believed everything we heard, we'd be suckered into all sorts of things. But sometimes we need to believe others. And most of all, we need to believe in what God tells us through his Word and his Spirit.

In John 20:24-31, Thomas doubts that Jesus really is alive until he sees Jesus in person. Jesus seldom appears to people visibly today, but we can believe he's alive because of others' testimonies, the Holy Spirit within us and the assurance we've been given in God's Word. Use this session to help your kids trust in Jesus as Thomas eventually did.

## ◆ Objectives

During this session kids will:
● experience being doubted;
● examine Thomas' doubting of Jesus;
● practice deciding who to believe; and
● express their belief in Jesus.

## ◆ Preparation

Read and study John 20:24-31.

Gather 3×5 cards, pencils, Bibles and copies of the "To Believe or Not to Believe" handout (page 67) for each person.

# The Session

## ◆ Dig

As kids arrive, give them each a 3×5 card and a pencil and have them write down the reason they came to the study. When everyone has arrived, gather all the cards and start reading the reasons aloud without revealing who wrote them. After reading each card, ask:

- **Do you believe that?**
- **Do you think someone here really came for that reason?**

Act skeptical about some of the reasons given. After going through all the cards, set them aside and ask:

- **How did it feel to be doubted?**

Say: **You may be wondering why I doubted some of your reasons for coming to this study. I wanted you to experience being doubted. We often doubt others, but it can be tough when others doubt us. Today we're going to be looking at doubt and belief.**

## ◆ Discover

Have someone read aloud John 20:24-29. Form groups of three or four to investigate the word "believe" in the passage. Pass out copies of the "To Believe or Not to Believe" handout (page 67) and have groups work through it.

When kids are finished, go over the handout together with the whole group. Ask:

- **What was Thomas' response when he finally saw Jesus?**
- **What role did Jesus have in Thomas' life?**
- **Do you think Thomas ever doubted Jesus again? Explain.**
- **What would it take for you never to doubt Jesus again?**

## ◆ Experience

Form two teams. Say: **We're going to play "We Doubt It." Each of you will have a chance to tell something about yourself** that's either true or false. The other team will try to guess if you're telling the truth. If they think you're lying, they'll say, "We doubt it." If they think you're telling the truth, they'll say, "We believe you." If you fool them, your team gets a point. If the other team guesses correctly, it gets one point.

Alternate teams until each person has had a chance to tell something. Tally the score and announce the winners.

Ask:

● **How did it feel trying to guess if someone was telling the truth?**

● **How is that like trying to decide whether to believe someone in real life?**

● **How is this game like trying to decide whether to believe what Jesus says? How is it different?**

Say: **Sometimes we aren't sure if we can believe people or not, because we can't always be sure of their honesty or sincerity. But we know we can always trust what Jesus says.**

## ◆ Grow

Ask:

● **What things help us know we can always believe in Jesus?**

After kids give suggestions, have someone read the rest of the passage, John 20:30-31.

Ask:

● **What reason does the author give for writing the Gospel of John?**

● **What does the author say is the result of believing in Jesus?**

● **What does it mean in a person's life to believe in Jesus?**

Encourage your kids to think about their relationship with Jesus and how sincerely they believe in him and what he says. Give them a few minutes of silence to think and pray.

## ◆ Go

Form a circle. Say: **Now is your chance to express your belief in Jesus. You can simply say, "I believe in Jesus," or you can** name something Jesus has said that you believe. For example, you might say, "I believe Jesus when he says he loves me." Or you can remain silent if you don't want to say anything.

Start the process by briefly telling of your belief in Jesus. Let others share, but don't pressure anyone. When it seems no one else wants to speak, close your session with prayer, thanking God for sending Jesus and for the knowledge that we can trust in him.

## TO BELIEVE OR NOT TO BELIEVE

## INSTRUCTIONS:

Study the word "believe" in John 20:24-29 by answering the following questions.

1. What reason did Thomas give for not believing? Do you think it was a good reason? Why or why not?

2. Why did the other disciples believe?

3. What things about Jesus do you find hard to believe sometimes?

4. What did Jesus say about believing in verses 27 and 29?

5. What can we learn about believing in Jesus from this passage?

# Resurrection Realities

## ◆ Theme: Resurrection (All Gospels)

Christianity is unique among the world's religions—because its leader is still alive! Other religious leaders thought they could point the way to eternal life, but Jesus said, "Come, follow me" (Mark 1:17). He went into the grave and came back to life again. We, too, will follow him into our own graves. But his promise and power assure us that we will not stay there. And even today, his resurrection power brings new life to the dead areas of our hearts.

Young people often feel they're immortal. But death is a reality that faces us all, even the young. This session will help kids come to grips with the truth of Christ's resurrection, and discover how his resurrection power can bring them new life today.

## ◆ Objectives

During this session kids will:
- study Bible passages about the Resurrection;
- explore key ideas for a talk on death and dying;
- experience puppets being "dead" and "alive"; and
- pray about one area of their lives that needs Christ's resurrection power.

## ◆ Preparation

Read and study the following gospel passages related to the Resurrection: Matthew 28:1-10; Mark 12:18-27; Luke 14:12-14; John 5:19-30 and 6:35-59; and Romans 6:3-5.

Gather a small candle, matches, pencils, Bibles, paper sacks and markers. Make a copy of the "Mortimer's Message" handout (page 72) for each person.

# The Session

## ◆ Dig

Hold up your candle and talk about trick candles. Mention how people try to blow them out, but they remain lighted. Say: **How many of you think this candle could be a trick candle? Let's find out if it is.**

Light your candle and ask a volunteer to blow it out. When the flame doesn't come back, ask:

● **Are you disappointed? Why or why not?**

● **How could blowing out the flame on this candle represent what it means to die?**

## ◆ Discover

Say: **Today we're going to see what the Bible says about Jesus' death—and what happened after his death. We'll look at key passages in the gospels that talk about Christ's resurrection. And we'll learn what the Resurrection has to do with us.**

Form groups of two or three and distribute pencils, Bibles and copies of the "Mortimer's Message" handout (page 72) to each person. Assign one or more of the passages on the handout to each group and allow about 10 minutes for kids to study their passages and fill in the outline.

When groups are finished, have them tell what they wrote. Then summarize with these discussion questions:

● **Is it easy to believe in Christ's resurrection? Why or why not?**

● **What evidence is there that Jesus actually rose from the dead?**

**69**

● How does the truth of Christ's resurrection affect the way you live? the way you face death?

Say: **Without Jesus' resurrection, there could be no "new life" in Christ. Because of Christ's physical resurrection, those of us who follow him have already become spiritually reborn. And that frees us to live a joy-filled new life in Christ.**

## ◆ Experience

Say: **Let's see what Christ's resurrection means for us.**

Form two teams. Give each person a paper sack and a marker. Tell kids to use their markers to create paper-sack puppets. Explain that they may decorate their puppets however they want, and that they'll use the puppets in a skit in a few minutes.

When the puppets are completed, have kids test them, then place them on the floor. Say to one of the groups: **On "go," I want each of you to take your puppet, find a puppet partner from the other group and do a puppet dance together while humming your favorite love song. However, you may not touch your puppet partner.**

Say to the other group: **On "go," the other group members will come over to you and try to dance with your puppets. But you may not pick up or touch your puppets in any way. Go!**

## ◆ Grow

Allow a few minutes for kids to try to get their puppets to dance with the lifeless puppets. Then call everyone together and ask:

● How did it feel to be a "live" puppet? Explain.

● How did it feel to be a "dead" puppet? Explain.

● How did it feel to try to dance with a "dead" puppet?

● How is using your arm to give life to a puppet like the way Christ's resurrection gives life to us?

● How are the "dead" puppets like people who don't know that Christ's resurrection can give them new life?

● How can we walk in the power of Christ's resurrection?

Say: **Without Christ, we are all spiritually dead. But when we become Christians, the power of Christ's resurrection** enters our hearts, and we have new life. As we obey God, we are able to live the new life Jesus offers.

##  Go

Say: **In a hidden place on your puppet, write one area of your life that Christ has resurrected. Also write one area of your life that feels dead—an area that you think still needs to be resurrected.**

When kids are finished, have someone read aloud Romans 6:3-5. Say: **Jesus' resurrection power is real today. We can celebrate his resurrection by thanking him for the ways his power has brought us new life. But we can also rejoice over the areas that still might feel dead—because we know that he'll bring new life to those areas too. Let's close by praying for the areas of our lives that need his resurrection power.**

Close with prayer, thanking God for Christ's resurrection and the new life it brings kids today. Ask him to breathe new life into the areas of kids' lives that still feel dead.

After the prayer, encourage kids to take home their puppets as reminders to let Christ's resurrection power fill their lives every day.

# MORTIMER'S MESSAGE

## INSTRUCTIONS:

Mortimer Mortician is a Christian who believes in the Resurrection. He has seen this belief in others make a difference in how they face the death of their loved ones. Mortimer has been invited to give a talk at your school on death and resurrection. He wants to have a part of his talk focus on the Bible's view of the topic.

Be Mortimer. Organize your thoughts for your talk, based on the gospel passages and outline below:

Passages to use:
1. Matthew 28:1-10 — the historical fact of Christ's resurrection
2. Mark 12:18-27 — mistaken ideas about the Resurrection
3. Luke 14:12-14 — the nature of true heavenly rewards
4. John 5:19-30 — people who get to be raised to life
5. John 6:35-59 — Jesus' power to raise us

Outline to fill in:
● Summary of what the Bible passage says:


● The main idea about the Resurrection in this passage:


● An important thing, from this passage, for a teenager to know:


● A personal example of why this message is important to me:

# These Men Are Not Drunk!

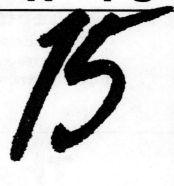

## ◆ Theme: Pentecost (Acts 2)

Powerful things happened on the day of Pentecost. How could the apostles have spoken so many different languages simultaneously? The crowd was perplexed, and some even thought the men were drunk because they appeared to babble like fools.

Peter bravely spoke out and challenged everyone to a new faith in the Lord Jesus Christ. The power of the Holy Spirit came upon him and the other apostles. His words were so powerful that 3,000 people joined the new church.

That same Holy Spirit is waiting to fill the lives of your students. Help them experience the joy and power of God's Spirit through this session.

## ◆ Objectives

During this session kids will:
- decide what determines whether someone is drunk;
- explore the events of the day of Pentecost;
- experience the effect of the Spirit's power on people's lives; and
- find ways to allow the Holy Spirit to guide their lives.

## ◆ Preparation

Read and study Acts 2.

Gather masking tape, pens, Bibles, an empty bottle, crepe paper, markers, a large electric fan and paper.

# The Session

## ◆ Dig

Form groups of six or fewer and give each group masking tape and a pen. Tell each group to choose one of its members to be "drunk," then identify what makes him or her appear drunk by writing the telltale signs on strips of masking tape and taping them to appropriate places on the drunk person's body.

When groups are finished, have each present its drunk person and explain the taped-on indicators. Read aloud Ephesians 5:18, then say: **Have you ever been so giddy or full of joy that people thought you were drunk? Well, today we're going to look at an event in scripture that was just like that—the day of Pentecost.**

## ◆ Discover

Have kids turn to Acts 2 and form a circle. Hold up an empty bottle and say: **We're going to play a variation of Spin the Bottle. I'll spin the bottle on the floor, and each time it points to you, you must read one verse from Acts 2. We'll continue until we've finished the chapter.**

After the reading, ask:

● **Why do you think some people thought the apostles were drunk?**

● **What would you have been thinking if you had been in that crowd?**

● Why do you think so many people made commitments to Christ that day?

● Does the Holy Spirit have the same influence today that he did on the day of Pentecost? Why or why not?

Say: **The Holy Spirit's power is just as real today as it was when Peter spoke. Let's look a little deeper at what the Holy Spirit can do in our lives.**

## ◆ Experience

Hand each person a strip of crepe paper and a marker, then gather in front of the electric fan. Have kids carefully write their names on their strips, then hold their strips in front of them. Ask:

● **What's happening to your strip right now?**

● **Does it seem alive or dead? Explain.**

Read aloud John 3:8, then turn on the fan. Allow kids to let their strips flutter freely in the breeze. Then ask:

● **What's happening to your strip now that the fan is on?**

● **Does it seem alive or dead? Explain.**

● **How is the wind's effect on your strip like the Spirit's effect on our lives?**

● **How is this experience like Pentecost?**

## ◆ Grow

Turn the fan off. Read John 3:8 aloud again, then ask:

● **What does it mean to be filled with the Spirit?**

● **Can what happened at Pentecost happen to you today? Why or why not?**

Say: **The Holy Spirit came at Pentecost and has been with us ever since. The Spirit's power has not changed, nor has his desire to fill our lives with his presence. And he can do that as we allow him the right to direct our lives.**

## ◆ Go

Say: **It's one thing to say you want the Holy Spirit to work in your life, and quite another to discern what that means practically for your day-to-day routine. Let's close by examining that issue.**

Give each person paper and a pen. Have kids read Acts 2:42-47. Say: **This passage gives us ideas about how we can allow the Holy Spirit to lead our lives more. From the passage write down three ways you can change your lifestyle to allow the Holy Spirit more control.**

When kids finish, have volunteers tell what they wrote. Close with prayer, asking God to change the lives of your kids through his Spirit.

# Turning Toward God

## ◆ Theme: Faith Commitment

(Acts 9:1-31)

Paul knew he'd been drastically transformed by the power of God. He constantly referred to God's grace and power as the source of his ability to accomplish great things for the kingdom of God.

In Acts 9 we see the beginning of Paul's transformation from a persecutor of the church to one of its key leaders. It took dramatic events to get Paul to change his direction. But those experiences apparently never lost their impact on him. In this session, kids will recognize the difference between just following God and being transformed by his power and grace. Use this session to help kids discover Christ's power in their own lives.

## ◆ Objectives:

During this session kids will:
● remember a time when their lives changed direction;
● explore Acts 9:1-31;
● experience seeing "the bigger picture";
● list dead-end streets kids encounter; and
● suggest ways of turning back to God.

## ◆ Preparation

Read and study Acts 9:1-31.

Gather construction paper, markers, Bibles, newsprint, 3×5 cards, pencils, a sheet of white paper and tape.

# The Session

## ◆ Dig

Distribute construction paper and markers. Ask kids to draw a U-turn road sign and inside it to write about a point in their lives when they changed their minds about something significant. For example, kids could write about beginning to like a food or music group they had previously "hated." Or they might write about becoming friends with someone they had previously disliked.

To make their explanations clear, have kids divide their signs into three sections: (1) their position *before* the turn, (2) their position *after* the turn and (3) what *caused* them to make the turn.

When the signs are complete, ask kids to explain what they wrote. Then ask:

● **Was making your change hard or easy? Explain.**

● **Why is it usually difficult to make a U-turn in attitude, opinion or action?**

● **What does it take to cause a person to make such a radical change?**

Say: **In today's session, we'll see an example of an incredible turnaround. Saul—who eventually became the Apostle Paul—was originally a ferocious enemy of the new Christian church. But something happened on one of his trips that made him completely change direction. Let's see what it was.**

## ◆ Discover

Form groups of four or fewer and give each group a Bible, newsprint and a marker. Have groups read Acts 9:1-31, then create a "road map" of the events that caused Saul to make his incredible turnaround. Encourage kids to creatively decorate their maps with road signs and directional arrows to illustrate the path Saul traveled.

When groups are finished writing, have them share what they wrote. Then ask:

● **How would you feel if you were thrown to the ground by**

**78**

an awesome flash of light, heard a voice from the clouds and were blinded all at once?

● Do you think Saul knew who was talking to him from heaven?

● Why do you think it took such a dramatic event to make Saul "see the light"?

Say: **Saul was convinced that he was doing the right thing, but God intervened to show him the "big picture." As a result, his life drastically changed. Let's try an experiment to see how our own perceptions of reality can be wrong.**

## ◆ Experience

Give kids each a 3×5 card and a pencil. With a black marker, make a small dot in the center of a white sheet of paper and hold it up for all to see. Tell kids to silently write on their cards what they see. Then tell kids you are going to check each card for the "right" answer. Have those with the right answer—"a sheet of paper"—move to a corner of the room and wait quietly. Don't accept any other answers. Most kids will have the "wrong answer"—a black dot.

Do a second round of this exercise to allow more of the kids to get it "right." Many will probably still miss the point.

After the second round, have the group with the right answer tell the others what they wrote. Then ask:

● **How did you feel when you were told you got the answer right? wrong?**

● **If you got the right answer on the second try, what caused your inner "light bulb" to turn on?**

● **How is this experience like what happened to Saul on the road to Damascus?**

● **How is it like when we can see only a small part of God's plan for our lives?**

Say: **Just as I changed your perception of reality in this exercise by causing you to see the whole sheet of paper, God invites people to change their perceptions of reality by living according to his perspective rather than their own.**

## ◆ Grow

Tape a sheet of newsprint to the wall. Across the top, write "Dead-End Streets for Kids." Have kids call out suggestions of "roads" teenagers are tempted to travel today—roads that lead them away from God. For example, kids might say, "taking drugs," "drinking" or "having sex before marriage."

After you have about 10 dead-end roads, have kids brainstorm what it would take for a teenager to make a U-turn toward God for help in each situation. Encourage practical solutions. Write kids' responses on newsprint.

## ◆ Go

Say: **Dead-end roads are all around us. Many of you face dead-end roads in your own lives. Let's close today by identifying some of those roads and committing to making a U-turn back to God.**

Give kids each a 3×5 card and a pencil. On their cards, have kids write one dead-end road they are currently facing in their lives. Form pairs and have partners pray about each other's dead-end road, challenging each other to commit to making a U-turn back to God.

When pairs are finished, close the session with prayer, thanking God for showing kids the bigger picture of life in Christ, and helping them make U-turns back to him.

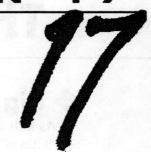

# The Power of Grace

## ◆ Theme: Grace (Romans 3:19-28)

In Romans 3 Paul explains the connection between the Law and grace. We need the Law to show us we've sinned, but there's no way the Law can save us. We've all sinned, and by the rules of the Law, we all deserve to be punished by eternal separation from God.

But the good news is that God's grace, apart from the Law, has provided the possibility for us to become acceptable to God—through faith in Jesus Christ. And God's grace is free!

Use this session to help your kids experience the freedom and learn the responsibility of receiving God's grace.

## ◆ Objectives

During this session kids will:
● feel the illogical nature of grace;
● discover what Romans 3 says about the benefits and requirements of the Law and grace;
● experience an example of grace; and
● offer thanks to God for specific benefits of his grace.

## ◆ Preparation

Read and study Romans 3:19-28.

Gather a candy bar, a marble, Bibles, pencils, M&M's candies and art supplies. Make a copy of the "Grace Quiz" handout (page 85) for each person.

You'll also need a chalkboard and chalk or newsprint and a marker.

# The Session

## ◆ Dig

As kids arrive, greet them warmly and offer them each a candy bar, but don't give them one unless they have a marble to give you in exchange. As the last person enters, offer the candy bar again, asking that person if he or she has a marble to exchange for it. When the person says no, produce a marble and give it to the person. Then ask again if the person has a marble to exchange for the candy bar. Make the exchange, then have the person sit down.

Ask:

● **How did you feel when I offered you the candy bar, but then required you to give me a marble in exchange for it?**

● **How did you feel when I gave (name) a marble so he (or she) could exchange it for the candy?**

● **Did you feel I treated you unfairly? Why or why not?**

Say: **What I did as you arrived was an example of Law and grace. You all needed a marble to get the candy bar, but none of you had a marble. That's like the Old Testament law. It offered people the chance to reach God if they could just follow the commands. But no one could.**

**I gave a marble to (name) so he (or she) could get the candy bar, even though (name) didn't have a marble to start with. That's like grace. Grace is God's free provision of what we need to have eternal life today. We're going to talk a lot about grace today.**

## ◆ Discover

Have kids take turns reading aloud successive verses from Romans 3:19-28. Ask:

● **What is the "Law" this passage is referring to?**

● **Why isn't the Law all we need to be like Jesus?**

● **From what you've read here, what makes a person right with God?**

Say: **The Law is like a standard that tries to change us from the outside in. That's why it could never really help us reach God—even if we changed our outward behavior to obey the Law, our hearts were still wrong.**

Grace works in just the opposite way. Instead of imposing a standard on us from the outside, it works on us from the inside out, changing our hearts so we naturally live up to God's requirements.

## ◆ Experience

Say: **Now we're going to take a little quiz to see how much you know about grace. If you all get every answer right, you'll all get M&M's candies. But if anyone misses even one answer, no one gets candy. No Bibles are allowed.**

Pass out copies of the "Grace Quiz" handout (page 85) and pencils.

Let kids groan about the last question for a minute or two, until it becomes clear that no one knows the answer. Then say: **Because I love you and want you to have the candy, I'll tell you this: The answer to the last question is "charis."**

The answer to the other four questions is "true."

Since you gave the answer to the last question, everyone should have all the questions right. Say: **You all got a perfect score. Here's your prize!**

Pass out the candy and let the kids enjoy it. Then ask:

● **How did you feel when you realized you weren't all going to have the right answers?**

● **How did you feel when I gave you the answer you lacked?**

● **How is what I did in giving you the answer and the candy similar to God's grace?**

● **What does it mean to receive God's grace in your own life?**

## ◆ Grow

Say: **Grace is God's free provision of what we need to have eternal life today. And receiving God's grace in our lives is without doubt the best thing that can happen to us. All we have to do is believe in Jesus and ask for God's grace.**

Have kids brainstorm a list of good things that come to them as a result of receiving God's grace. Kids might say things such as, "eternal life with God," "the power to say no to wrong behavior," "God's blessings" or "God's presence in our lives."

Record kids' responses on a chalkboard or newsprint. Encourage kids to keep going until you have a list of at least 10 things. Then ask:

● **Without God's grace, what would be different in our lives?**

● **How will this study change the way you live your life?**

Read aloud 2 Peter 1:2-3. Then say: **When we realize how abundant God's grace is toward us, we can move beyond fear and walk in the joy of knowing God's love for us.**

 **Go**

Form pairs and hand out whatever art supplies you have available. Have each pair choose one thing from the list of the benefits of God's grace and create something expressing their thanks to God for that particular thing. When they're finished, have kids present their creations to the group. Display the creations around the room for the next few weeks as reminders of God's grace.

To close your session, have pairs hold up their creations to God and say sentence prayers of thanks to God for his grace.

# GRACE QUIZ

## INSTRUCTIONS:

Answer each of the following questions.

True or False:

1. Paul talks about grace and law in Romans 3. _____

2. Grace comes to us because of our faith in Jesus. _____

3. The Old Testament law can be found in the Old Testament. _____

4. Grace is God's free provision of what we need to
have eternal life today. _____

Fill in the blank:

5. The Greek word for grace is _____.

# We Hope!

## ◆ Theme: Hope in Hard Times
(Romans 8:18-30)

In Romans 8, Paul helps Christians put their troubles in perspective. No matter how hard it gets, he says, we can always remember the wonderful future we have in store for us. And not only that, but we have the Holy Spirit with us to help us when things get tough now.

However things seem, we have God's promise that everything works together for our good. Even though what we face is sometimes hard to understand, in light of that promise we can always trust that God is in control. Use this session to help your kids trust God in tough times and lean on the hope we all have in Jesus.

## ◆ Objectives
During this session kids will:
● discuss what motivates people to keep going;
● define "hope" based on Romans 8:18-30;
● experience how hope can keep them going in hard times; and
● choose scripture verses to lean on when troubles come.

## ◆ Preparation
Read and study Romans 8:18-30.

Collect newspaper or magazine reports of people winning lotteries. Gather paper, pencils, Bibles, masking tape, paper cups, marbles and colored paper. Choose a prize to offer for the Experience section, such as a dollar bill or a favorite candy.

# The Session

## ◆ Dig

When you're ready to begin, pass out the lottery articles and have kids read and briefly summarize them. Then ask:

● **What are the odds of winning the big prize in one of these lotteries?**

● **For each dollar spent on lottery tickets, how much money is awarded in prizes?**

If kids don't know, tell them that in most lotteries about half of the money taken in is awarded in prizes. Then ask:

● **Why do people play lotteries?**

Say: **People play lotteries because of the hope they have of winning the big prize. They hope that someday they'll become millionaires by winning the big one. The odds are that they'll spend more money on tickets than they'll ever win in a drawing. But that little bit of hope keeps them buying.**

Today we're going to talk about having hope in hard times. And we'll see how the kind of hope God offers is a lot better than the hope that keeps people interested in lotteries.

## ◆ Discover

Form four groups. (A group can be as small as one person.) Give groups paper and pencils, and assign them each one of these passages: Romans 8:18-21; 8:22-25; 8:26-27; 8:28-30.

Say: **You're all in a foreign language class. The word "hope" is new to you, and your instructor has given you your assigned passage to help you understand this word. From your passage alone, write a definition of "hope."**

Give groups a few minutes to read over their passages and form definitions. Then have them report their definitions to the whole group. After the reports, ask:

● **Why did we come up with such different definitions of hope?**

**87**

● **Is one definition more nearly correct than the others? Explain.**

● **What, then, is hope?**

Work together to come up with a definition of hope that encompasses at least parts of all the definitions the groups presented.

## ◆ Experience

Hold up the prize you've chosen and let kids know that the winner of the next activity gets to keep the prize. Make a line across the floor on one end of your room with a strip of masking tape. At the other end of the room place one empty paper cup for every two people participating. Then give each person a marble and have them all kneel behind the tape line.

Say: **The object of this game is to get your marble in a paper cup at the other end of the room and to set the paper cup upright. The catch is that you must keep your hands behind your back and may touch the marble and the cup only with your nose. You may also use your nose to keep someone else from winning. Remember, the winner in this game gets the prize!**

On "go" begin the game. If it appears that kids are going to win quickly, do something to stop them, like kicking their marbles away or dumping the marbles out of the cups before they can turn them upright. After several minutes of frustration, let someone win or declare the end of the game. Ask:

● **How did it feel trying to get the marble in the cup?**

● **What kept you going in this game when it was so tough?**

● **How is that like how our hope in Christ keeps us going when things get tough in the Christian life?**

● **How does your Christian hope change the way you live your life?**

## ◆ Grow

Say: **There are times when we need to lean on that hope more than other times. When things are going well, it's easy not to think about the future. But when things aren't going so well, sometimes we need to think about the hope we have to keep us going.**

Ask:

● **What tough situations do you face in your life that would be easier if you were to think about the hope you have for the future?**

Have kids tell about tough times they've had as Christians, such as specific times of temptation. Start the sharing with an example of your own.

After several have shared, say: **In tough times, it's good to have scripture to lean on to remind us of the hope we have. Now we're going to choose a few scriptures to keep with us to lean on.**

 **Go**

Pass out pieces of colored paper and have kids tear their papers into shapes representing hope. Then let kids show and explain their symbols.

Have kids review the scripture passage and each choose one key verse that sums up how their hope in Christ affects their lives.

When kids have each chosen a verse, have them write it on their torn-paper shape and share it with the rest of the group.

Encourage kids to keep their shapes with them to refer to when the going gets tough.

Close the session with prayer, thanking God for the hope he gives and asking him to help kids lean on his Word in difficult times.

# Love: The Truth Unmasked!

## ◆ Theme: True Love (1 Corinthians 13)

"Love" is one of the most misused words in the English language. With it, we describe our longing for those dearest to our hearts, as well as our feelings toward the latest fashion trend. It's no wonder people struggle to understand what love is and how to find it.

This session gives kids a vital look at God's perspective on the nature of true love. As the author of love, God is uniquely qualified to help kids understand the beauty—and cost—of true love.

## ◆ Objectives

In this session kids will:
- race to list things they love;
- discuss the qualities of love found in 1 Corinthians 13;
- view a pincushion as a symbol of love's persistence; and
- measure their own ability to love against the biblical standard.

## ◆ Preparation

Read and study 1 Corinthians 13.

You'll need paper, pencils, tape, newsprint, markers, Bibles, straight pins and a pincushion or sponge. For each person you'll also need a copy of the "Choose Love" handout (page 94).

# The Session

## ◆ Dig

Give each person a sheet of paper and a pencil. On "go," have them each list as many things they "love" as they can in one minute. After the minute is up, have volunteers tell what they wrote. Point out the diversity in things they love. Then say: **Love can mean many different things, can't it? It's no wonder most people struggle so much with what love really is. Fortunately for Christians, God has given us a description of true love in 1 Corinthians 13. But beware! What we find there may surprise you!**

## ◆ Discover

Tape a sheet of newsprint to the wall. On it, write the word "LOVE" in big block letters. (See the example below.)

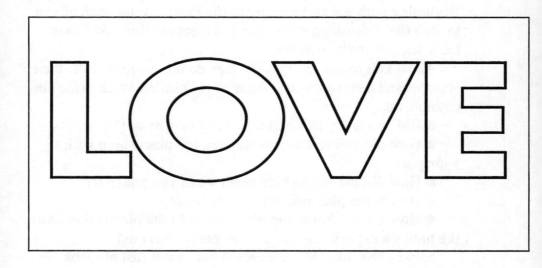

Form four groups and assign each group one of these passages: 1 Corinthians 13:1-3; 1 Corinthians 13:4-5; 1 Corinthians 13:6-7; and 1 Corinthians 13:8-13. Have each group read its passage and find the qualities of love listed there. Assign each group a different letter in the word "LOVE," and have groups use markers to write the qualities they find in the appropriate letter.

After groups have listed love's qualities, have them explain their responses. Then ask:

● **Of all the qualities listed here, what do you think is love's most important quality?**

● **How does it make you feel when you see all these standards for what true love is?**

● **Can you live up to these standards? Why or why not?**

Say: **True love isn't quite as easy as you might have thought, is it? In fact, God's standards for true love may seem beyond our reach. In a moment, we'll see how we can live up to God's standards for true love. But first, let's look more closely at what true love really means.**

# ◆ Experience

Give kids each a straight pin and have them form a circle around a table. Set a large pincushion or sponge on the table. Say: **Beginning with me and moving to the right, I want each of you to stab the pincushion with your pin a couple times and then leave the pin in the cushion.**

Allow kids to talk freely while they do this exercise. Note their attitudes and their comments. After all the pins are stuck in the pin cushion, ask:

● **Did you enjoy this activity? Why or why not?**

● **How did you feel as you stabbed the pincushion with your pin?**

● **How did the pincushion react when you poked it?**

● **How is the pincushion like true love?**

● **How are the holes and pins we left in the pincushion like the pain we experience when other people hurt us?**

Say: **Love is like this pincushion because it just absorbs whatever blows or stabs it receives. And because God has planted his love in us, all Christians have the ability to love**

**92**

with the same consistency the pincushion had when we stabbed it with pins.

## ◆ Grow

Give each person a Bible, a pencil and a copy of the "Choose Love" handout (page 94). Have kids refer to 1 Corinthians 13:4-7 to fill in the blanks on the handout. When kids are finished, have them each write their name at the top of the page.

Have kids read aloud the handout in unison. Then say: **Reading this passage in this way is challenging, isn't it? Loving others in this way may seem out of reach to you. But by drawing from Christ's love in your heart, you can become his "love connection" in your friendships and your family.**

Encourage kids to take their handouts home and tape them to their bedroom mirrors as a reminder to always "choose love."

## ◆ Go

Have kids return to a circle around the pincushion. Say: **Today we've learned that true love is much more costly than most people think, and we've seen that God is able to help us consistently love others in that way. Let's close by expressing love to each other using the pincushion we stabbed with pins earlier.**

Have kids pass the pincushion around the circle. As each person holds the pincushion, have him or her say one thing he or she appreciates about another person in the circle without mentioning that person's name. Then have the speaker pass the pincushion to the person he or she was talking about. Have that person continue by saying something he or she appreciates about another person in the circle, and passing the pincushion to that person. Continue until everyone has held the pincushion at least once, preferably twice if you have time. Make sure no one is left out.

Close with prayer, thanking God for the love he asks kids to show to him and others.

# CHOOSE LOVE

Name: _____

**Instructions:** Use 1 Corinthians 13:4-7 to fill in the missing words in the "I" below. As you do, think about how well your life measures up to God's description of true love.

I am _____ and _____.
I am not _____,
I do not _____, and I
am not _____.
I am not _____,
I am not _____,
and I do not _____.
I do not count up _____
_____. I am not
happy with _____,
but I am happy with _____
_____; I _____
_____ all things. I
always _____, always
_____, and always _____.*

*A paraphrase of the New Century Version.

# Treasure In Clay Jars

## ◆ Theme: Self-Esteem
(2 Corinthians 4:7-15)

Many teenagers struggle with low self-esteem. Too often, pressures are placed on them to be someone or something they really aren't. But in 2 Corinthians, Paul helps us see how Christians have great value because of a "treasure" God has placed in each of us.

Use this session to help kids see God's treasure within them.

## ◆ Objectives

During this session kids will:
- play a game while looking in mirrors;
- explore how they feel about being God's "earthen vessels";
- examine their uniqueness and value as people; and
- write one thing they appreciate about another group member.

## ◆ Preparation

Read and study 2 Corinthians 4:7-15.

Gather mirrors, newsprint, markers, modeling clay, a Bible and pencils. Make a copy of the "Fine Folding Flinging Thing" handout (page 99) for each person.

# The Session

## ◆ Dig

Form teams of no more than five. Give teams each a similar-size mirror. Place a sheet of newsprint at one end of the room for each team. Have teams line up across from their sheets of newsprint. Give the first person on each team a mirror and a marker.

Say: **On "go," you must race backward, using the mirror to guide you, to your team's newsprint. Then you must print your first name on the newsprint. You may not turn to face the newsprint but must write behind your back, again using the mirror to guide you. When you're finished, you may look at your name. If any letters are backward, you must start again, still using the mirror. When you've written your name right, run back to your team and hand the marker and mirror to the next person in line. We'll go until one team is completely finished.**

Start the game. After a team wins, congratulate everyone.

Say: **In this game, we spent a lot of time looking in mirrors. In life—kind of like in this activity—we sometimes have a rough time liking and dealing with what we see in mirrors. But today we're going to see how God gives each of us a unique beauty that makes us important and valuable.**

## ◆ Discover

Give each person a clump of modeling clay. Read aloud 2 Corinthians 4:7-15. Say: **Form your clay into a shape that represents how you feel as God's "jars of clay."**

When kids are finished, have volunteers explain their creations. Then ask:

● **What does this passage tell us about what it means to be God's children?**

● **What is the treasure we have in ourselves?**

● **How are our talents and abilities also like "treasures"?**

**96**

Say: **Imagine your clay is the form God created you to be. Find a partner and tell him or her what unique abilities or gifts God has given your clay form.**

After a couple minutes, call time. Have volunteers tell what they talked about with their partners. Then display the clay for the rest of the class as a reminder of the message in the scripture passage.

## ◆ Experience

Give kids each a copy of the "Fine Folding Flinging Thing" handout (page 99). Say: **This handout has many different solid and dotted lines on it. Take a couple minutes to fold and tear your handout into anything you want using these lines as a guide. You can use as many or as few of the lines as you want. Don't look at other people's papers. Create something only you can create.**

After a few minutes, form groups of no more than four. Have kids each show their completed "Fine Folding Flinging Thing" to the rest of their group and describe why they chose to fold and tear it they way they did.

## ◆ Grow

Read aloud the following questions, giving groups a minute or two to discuss each one:

● **Did everyone choose to fold their paper the same way? Why or why not?**

● **How do you feel about the way your paper is folded compared to the other group members' papers?**

● **How is that like the way people feel when comparing themselves to others?**

● **What is unique about each person's paper?**

● **What is unique about each person in your group? (Say only positive things, please.)**

● **How is the uniqueness of each "Fine Folding Flinging Thing" like the uniqueness of each person in the room?**

● **How does it feel to be God's creation?**

**Go**

Say: **Paul reminds us that our earthly bodies are God's handiwork. We can be thankful that God has made each of us unique and full of gifts.**

Form a circle and give each person a pencil. Have kids each determine who is the third person to their right, then write that person's name on their "Fine Folding Flinging Thing."

Say: **Write one thing you can thank God for about the person whose name is on your paper. Then "fling" that paper over to him or her. Read the message you receive as encouragement to be all God has made you to be.**

When kids have each received a paper and read it, close in a moment of silent prayer.

# FINE FOLDING FLINGING THING

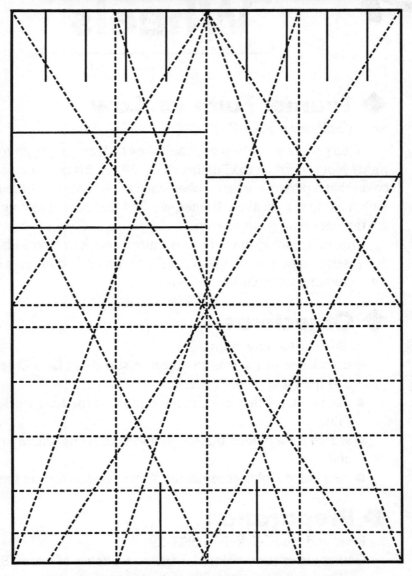

# Training Wheels

## ◆ Theme: Faith vs. Law

(Galatians 3:21-29)

Nice people go to heaven, don't they? Mean people go to hell, right? Not according to Galatians 3:21-29. In this passage, we discover that a person's general obedience to the Law has little to do with making it to heaven. Rather, we find that people having faith are the ones who go to heaven.

This information may come as quite a shock to your kids. Use this session to help them understand why doing good things in no way guarantees eternal life.

## ◆ Objectives

In this session kids will:
- use plaster of Paris as an object lesson about faith in Jesus and the Law;
- discuss items that work in the same way the Law works with faith;
- search for a hidden treasure without knowing where to start; and
- take home a plaster reminder of their freedom from the Law.

## ◆ Preparation

Read and study Galatians 3:21-29.

Gather paper cups, colored markers, a pitcher of water, Bibles, paper plates and spoons. You'll also need enough plaster of Paris to give each person a cupful of the mix.

Make a copy of the "Hidden Treasure!" handout (page 104) for each person.

---

# The Session

---

## ◆ Dig

As kids arrive, give them each a paper cup and a marker. Have kids write their initials on their cups. Set out a pitcher of water and a bowl containing plaster of Paris. Help each person mix a cupful of plaster of Paris with the appropriate amount of water.

Say: **Today we're going to see how the Old Testament law is similar to your paper cups holding the plaster.**

When all the cups are filled, have kids place their cups against a wall on one side of the room.

## ◆ Discover

After the cups have all been set in a safe place, say: **Today we're going to see what role the Old Testament law plays in our lives as New Testament Christians. But before I give you any hints, I want you to try to tackle this issue on your own.**

Form three groups and have each group read Galatians 3:21-29. Then assign each group one of these items:

● training wheels on a bicycle

● gelatin chilled in a gelatin mold

● a protective elastic harness for a gymnast in training

Have each group study its passage, then decide how the Old Testament law is "like" their assigned item. Encourage kids to thoroughly explain their responses.

After all the groups have responded, say: **Each of your items had one thing in common. Each is an item that is essential for guidance and safety at the beginning, but later—once it's**

**101**

served its purpose—can be set aside. In the same way, the Old Testament law is essential to help guide us to Jesus, but as Christ takes charge of our lives, we come to depend on his grace rather than the old written Law to bring us life.

# ◆ Experience

Say: **Let's see what might've happened if we'd never received the Law.**

Have kids stand at random locations all around the room. Give kids each a copy of the "Hidden Treasure!" handout (page 104) and have them follow the handout's instructions. Kids may complain that the handout doesn't provide enough information, but just encourage them to do what it says.

After everyone has followed the instructions, call everyone together and ask:

● **Why didn't anyone find the treasure?**

● **What did you find?**

● **What information did you need for the directions to be useful?**

Say: **You needed to know where to stand at the beginning before you could even begin to hope to find the treasure.**

Ask:

● **How is this experience similar to what it might be like to try to find Jesus if the Law had never been given?**

Say: **Everyone needs to find God. But without God's help, we don't know where to begin, just like you didn't know where to begin your treasure hunt. The Old Testament law shows us where to begin our search for God, and it points the way to Jesus, who is our "hidden treasure."**

# ◆ Grow

Say: **Let's check our plaster cups to see how they're doing.**

Have kids retrieve their cups of plaster and give them each a paper plate. Have kids remove their formed plaster from the paper molds and set them on the plates. Ask:

● **At the beginning of the session, I said we'd discover how your paper cups are similar to the Old Testament law. Now** can any of you guess how they are similar?

Say: **The paper cup acted as a mold for the plaster while it was still unformed. Once the plaster became solid, it kept its shape even when the cup was removed. In the same way, the Law guides us to understand what the Christian life "looks" like. But once Christ enters our lives, he writes his law on our hearts and helps us do what's right even when the external Law is removed.**

##  Go

Set out several colored markers. Read aloud Romans 8:1-4 and say: **Let's symbolize our freedom from the Old Testament law by writing this scripture reference on our plaster shapes and decorating them.**

Have kids write "Romans 8:1-4" on their plasters, then decorate their new creations with the colored markers. Encourage kids to take their plasters home as a reminder that they are free from the law. Close with prayer, thanking God for sending Christ to free kids from life under the Law.

# HIDDEN TREASURE!

## INSTRUCTIONS:

Follow these directions to locate an exciting hidden treasure.

1. Take three steps forward.

2. Turn right.

3. Take two steps backward.

4. Turn left.

5. Take eight steps forward.

6. Turn left twice.

7. Take two steps forward.

8. Take five steps sideways to the left.

9. Bend over.

10. Pick up the treasure!

# Matches Made in Heaven

## ◆ Theme: Married Life

(Ephesians 5:21-28)

Many people claim the Bible is no longer relevant when it comes to marriage. Many women believe the Bible instructs them to live their lives cowering under the authority of their husbands. And men, too, are turned off when they think the Bible tells them to look for wives who are servants rather than equals.

But is that really the picture scripture paints of what marriage is all about? Hardly.

As Christians, we need to understand what the Bible really says about marriage—which was God's idea in the first place. This session explores the scriptural truths about the marriage relationship and helps kids get a handle on how those truths might apply to their future (or present) lives.

## ◆ Objectives

During this session kids will:
● discuss their expectations of a future spouse;
● share opinions about what makes a marriage work;
● experience how it feels to be the "ideal" spouse; and
● identify one positive quality they'll bring to a marriage.

## ◆ Preparation

Read and study Ephesians 5:21-28.

Gather light pink and light blue construction paper, masking tape, markers, Bibles and a wedding ring.

# The Session

## ◆ Dig

Form two groups—one of guys and the other of girls. It's okay if the groups are uneven. Give the guys' group light pink construction paper, tape and a marker. Give the girls' group light blue construction paper, tape and a marker.

Say: **Today we're going to talk about marriage and married life. I know you'll have lots of opinions on this topic, so let's get started. Appoint one person in your group to be the other group's "mannequin." Brainstorm all the words or phrases you would use to describe the perfect spouse. Write each one on a sheet of construction paper and tape it to the mannequin. Try to completely cover that person. Go to work.**

When the groups are ready, stand the mannequins in front of them and have each group explain what it wrote. Ask:

● **How do you feel about the other group members' description of the perfect spouse?**

● **Why are these things important?**

Say: **Paul once wrote to the church at Ephesus about how husbands and wives are supposed to get along. I wonder how his words will fit with your descriptions of the ideal spouse.**

## ◆ Discover

Without removing the paper from the first mannequins, have each group choose a second mannequin. Tell groups to read

Ephesians 5:21-28 and create a new composite of the ideal spouse on the second mannequin. But this time, have kids base their descriptions solely on the information in the passage.

When groups are finished, have all four mannequins stand next to each other. Have kids compare their first descriptions with their second. Ask:

● **What's the greatest similarity between the first and second descriptions?**

● **What's the biggest difference?**

● **Would you like a spouse like the one described in the passage? Why or why not?**

● **After looking at all these composites, what would you say is the most important quality for your spouse to have?**

Say: **Having the ideal spouse the Bible describes would be awesome, wouldn't it? But let's see how you feel when we turn the tables on you. Let's see how you would like being the ideal spouse to your husband or wife.**

# ◆ Experience

Hand out Bibles and line up guys and girls facing each other. Have each person select one person from the other group to focus on. It's okay if someone has more than one person focused on him or her. Say: **Turn to Ephesians 5. I'm going to ask each group to do some things related to this passage. You can't argue with me. Just follow the directions. We'll discuss your feelings when the experience is over.**

Follow this sequence:

● Tell the guys to read verse 22 loudly at the girls.

● Tell the girls to get on their knees in front of the guys.

● Tell the guys to read verse 23.

● Tell the girls to grab the guys around their ankles as if they were worshiping them.

● Tell the guys to read verse 24.

● Tell the girls to bow down to the guys.

Say: **Girls, it's your turn. Stand up and turn to Ephesians 5.**

● Tell the girls to read verse 25 loudly.

● Tell the guys to stand beside the girls and look as though they're protecting them.

**107**

● Tell the girls to read verses 26 and 27.

● Tell the guys to bow down, cup their hands and lift them toward the girls as though offering them water.

● Tell the girls to read verse 28.

● Tell the guys to kiss the girls' feet.

## ◆ Grow

After the experience, gather in a circle and ask:

● **How did it feel to act out this passage?**

● **What did you like about it? dislike about it?**

● **What do you think Paul really meant to say to husbands and wives?**

● **What do you think it means to "submit" to each other in love and respect?**

● **What are some ways you've seen submission work in couples' lives?**

● **Did you like what you saw? Why or why not?**

Say: **If we compare this passage to the way the church relates to Christ, then it all makes sense. Christ's role is to lay down his life for the church, just as the husband is to lay down his life and serve his wife. In that context, the wife is to allow herself to fall under her husband's protection, just as the church is to submit to Christ.**

## ◆ Go

Say: **According to scripture, it takes two people to make a marriage work. Each person has a different role, but neither role is more important than the other. Let's close by identifying qualities and attitudes referred to in Ephesians that can help make a marriage strong.**

Read aloud Ephesians 5:22-28 again. Have kids each think of one quality or attitude from the passage that they could bring to a marriage to make it strong. Say: **I'm holding in my hand a wedding ring. It's the symbol a man and woman give one another to bind their relationship. We'll pass it around the circle as we talk about the qualities you've thought of.**

Pass the ring around the circle and have each person tell the

**108**

biblical quality he or she could bring to a marriage. After everyone has spoken, close with prayer, asking God to bless your group with strong, healthy marriages founded on the truths of scripture.

# 23 The Greatest Hero

## ◆ Theme: Being Like Jesus
(Philippians 2:5-11)

Heroes are everywhere in today's world—in the latest movies, the hottest TV shows and gracing the covers of popular magazines. But are these bigger-than-life characters really "heroes"?

Philippians 2:5-11 portrays another kind of hero. But he doesn't wear cool shades or carry a big gun. About the only thing this hero has in common with a popular media hero is that he does say, "I'll be back."

His name is Jesus.

## ◆ Objectives
During this session kids will:
- play or be rescued by "heroes" in a game;
- explore how Jesus is a hero;
- experience the humility of being under others' control; and
- commit to being more Christlike.

## ◆ Preparation
Read and study Philippians 2:5-11.
Gather masking tape, rope, blankets and Bibles.

# The Session

## ◆ Dig

Form teams of six or fewer. Have one person on each team stand at one end of the room and the other members stand opposite their teammate.

Place a masking tape line two feet in front of the players standing by themselves. Then give a rope at least as long as the distance between the individual players and their teammates to each individual player. Place one blanket next to each team.

Say: **The individual players will be our "heroes" in this game. All of the other people on each team are on a sinking life raft surrounded by sharks. When I say "go," the heroes are to toss the ropes to their life rafts and pull one or more people sitting on the blankets to safety (past the masking-tape line) before the life raft sinks (I call time). The team with the most saved people will win. Only the hero may pull people to safety.**

When one team has gotten all its members to safety (or a couple minutes have passed), call time. Ask:

● **How did you heroes feel about your role in this game?**

● **How is the way we portrayed a hero like or unlike the way our world portrays heroes?**

## ◆ Discover

Have kids call out names of popular heroes in the media and describe why they're heroes.

Then say: **The Bible gives us a different picture of what a hero is. Let's take a look at what Paul had to say in Philippians about someone who became a true hero.**

Have a volunteer read aloud Philippians 2:5-11. Then ask:

● **What surprised you about this passage?**

● **How is this a portrait of a hero?**

Form trios and have teenagers read through the passage again, then take turns completing the following sentences:

**111**

● Jesus is a hero because ...

● What makes Jesus different from today's media heroes is...

● One way I can be more like Jesus is ...

# ◆ Experience

Say: To see Jesus as a hero is to see him as our role model. As Christians, we're to do our best to be like this hero, Jesus. Let's do an activity to help us understand more about Christ as our role model.

Form groups of seven. If you have a small group, ask your adult volunteers to assist you in this activity. Tell kids they're going to take turns falling into their groups' arms and being lifted high overhead. Have groups each decide which member will go first, then have the other members of each group line up facing each other, three on one side and three on the other. Have the remaining member of the group stand at one end of the line with his or her back to the group.

Say to those who are going first: On "go," I want you to close your eyes and fall backward into your group's arms. Once they're holding you, they'll lift you high overhead, then slowly lower you all the way to the floor, rocking you gently back and forth like a leaf in the wind. Ready, set, go!

Have the group members rotate positions until everyone has had a chance to be lifted and lowered by the others.

# ◆ Grow

After everyone has "fallen," ask:

● How did you feel as you fell and were lifted up by your group?

● How did it feel to catch and lift the other group members?

● How was falling backward into your group like humbling yourself before God and others?

● How was what your group did to you like what God does to those who humble themselves before him?

● From the passage we read earlier and from this activity, what do you think it means to humble yourself?

**112**

● **How can we humble ourselves to be more like Jesus?**

Say: **We humble ourselves just like Christ did—by serving others. If we put others first, God will exalt us at the proper time. By being like Jesus, we become heroes for God!**

 **Go**

Give kids each a Bible and have them find a quiet place in the room to read Philippians 2:5-11 silently. Encourage kids to consider what commitment they might make to becoming more Christlike. After a few minutes, call everyone together and have teenagers each say a one-sentence prayer thanking God for sending Jesus to be their hero or asking God to help them be more like Jesus.

# The Good Life

### ◆ Theme: Christian Lifestyle
(Colossians 3:1-17)

Colossians 3 gives new Christians lots of guidelines for living the new life in Christ. God didn't give us these guidelines to keep us from having fun. He gave them to help us live lives that are both pleasing to him and fulfilling for us.

Use this session to help your kids see that God's guidelines are meant to help us and that walking in God's love is the best way to live.

### ◆ Objectives
During this session kids will:
● think about how new life in Christ changes people;
● formulate guidelines for living from Colossians 3:1-17;
● experience the frustration of playing a game without rules; and
● thank God for guidelines that help them deal with problems they face daily.

### ◆ Preparation
Read and study Colossians 3:1-17.

Gather masking tape, newsprint, colored markers, Bibles, a chalkboard, chalk and three small foam balls.

# The Session

## ◆ Dig

Form groups of four or fewer and give each group masking tape, newsprint and colored markers. Tell groups they each have five minutes to transform one of their members into a butterfly using the materials you've provided.

After five minutes, call time and have each group present its butterfly person. Congratulate groups on their efforts and award honorary titles such as "Most Creative," "Most Realistic" and "Most Unlike a Butterfly."

Say: **Imagine you're a new butterfly. Yesterday you were a happy-go-lucky caterpillar, minding your own business. But now you've just emerged from your cocoon with these big, clumsy things attached to your back. Surely there must be some mistake. What are you supposed to do with these things? Your whole body seems different. Suddenly the rules for your life have changed.**

Ask:

● **How have the rules for your life changed since you changed from a caterpillar to a butterfly?**

● **What can you do now that you couldn't before?**

● **What could you do before that you can't now?**

● **How is this like the way people change when they experience new life in Christ?**

Say: **In this session we're going to be talking about the changes that take place when we receive new life in Christ—and about new guidelines we follow as we try to become more like him.**

## ◆ Discover

Have kids stay in their groups. Say: **You've been chosen as a member of the Reader's Digest Condensed Version Team to work on condensing the guidelines for living the Christian life**

**115**

as found in Colossians 3:1-17. **What your group needs to do is carefully read through the passage and formulate three or four general guidelines that cover the commands Paul gives in this passage.**

After groups have carefully read the passage and created their guidelines, have them present what they've created. List the guidelines on a chalkboard or newsprint. Then ask:

● **How do these guidelines apply to us today?**

● **What specific guidelines from the passage seem to fit best with things we face today?**

● **Why do we need guidelines like this?**

# ◆ Experience

Form three teams. Give each team a small foam ball and say: **We're going to play a little game. Ready, set, go!**

If teams don't start doing something, prod them. But don't give any instructions. Let kids try to figure out what they're supposed to do with the balls.

After a few minutes of frustration, stop the activity and call the kids together. Ask:

● **How did you feel playing this game?**

● **What made the game difficult?**

● **How might this be similar to trying to live a Christian life without any guidelines?**

● **Why did God give us guidelines in the Bible?**

# ◆ Grow

Say: **God gave us these guidelines to help us know how to please him. When we love him in response to his love for us, it's natural to seek to please him in our lives. That's where Paul's guidelines in Colossians 3 come in.**

Form two groups. Assign one group Colossians 3:1-11 and the other group 3:12-17. Have groups each choose three specific guidelines given in their verses that they feel are most applicable to teenage life today. The guidelines must be more specific than those discussed in the Discover section and must apply directly to kids' lives. Have groups put those guidelines into terms kids might use.

Have kids report on what they've found, then ask:

● **How might these guidelines help you live a better Christian life right now?**

# ◆ Go

Say: **This passage gives us one general guideline that sort of takes in all of the others.**

Read aloud Colossians 3:17. Ask:

● **How can everything we say and do be done for Jesus?**

Let several kids respond to this question, then say: **The last part of that verse tells us to give thanks to God in all we do. Let's close our session by doing a bit of thanking right now.**

Go back over the general and specific guidelines kids have studied in this session. Encourage kids to thank God in brief prayers for particular guidelines that seem most helpful. Close your prayer time with a thankful prayer of your own.

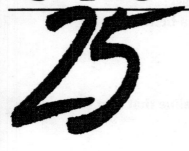

# Ready for the Big Date?

## ◆ Theme: Jesus' Return
(1 Thessalonians 5:1-11)

Acts 17 records the infancy of the Thessalonian church. Paul began by teaching in the Jewish synagogue. Over time, "Some of the Jews were persuaded and joined Paul and Silas, as did a large number of God-fearing Greeks and not a few prominent women" (Acts 17:4).

Persecution followed Paul's success. The persecution didn't let up after Paul left town, either. The letters Paul wrote to the Thessalonians acknowledge great temptation and persecution there. One of Paul's key themes is the encouragement a believer can find through the hope of Christ's return to earth.

How to be ready for that day has been a concern for Christians ever since. This session offers some practical advice on the subject.

## ◆ Objectives
During this session kids will:
● examine 1 Thessalonians 5:1-11;
● consider the effort it takes to get ready for "a big event";
● experience the frustration of not being ready to receive a treat; and
● prioritize their own activities with a view to Christ's return.

# ◆ Preparation

Read and study 1 Thessalonians 5:1-11.

Gather paper, pencils, Bibles, markers or crayons, and two large bags of M&M's candies.

For the Experience section, you'll need two flashlights with the batteries removed. You'll also need two sets of batteries that fit each flashlight. One set should be dead, the other fresh. Make sure the room will be dark when the lights are off.

---

# The Session

---

# ◆ Dig

Form two groups—guys in one, girls in the other. It's okay if the groups are uneven. Give a sheet of paper and a pencil to each group. Say: **Everyone has "big events" in life—such as that big date with your "special someone." As a group, make a list of all the things you go through—guys as guys, girls as girls—to get ready for that important date.**

After the lists are made, have the groups swap lists. Have each group elect a spokesperson. Have the spokesperson call out the items on the list as his or her group acts out the other group's list. After the "performances," ask:

● **On an effort scale of 1 to 10, with 1 being "hardly any effort" and 10 being "total effort," how much effort would you say most teenagers spend on getting ready for an important date? Why?**

● **On the same scale, how much effort would you say most teenagers spend on getting ready to meet God? Why?**

# ◆ Discover

Say: **No one knows how much time they have left in life. Jesus himself said no man could know the exact time he'd return. So we can't say with certainty just when anyone will have that "important date" with God. But the Apostle Paul gave great advice on what to do to be ready for that date.**

Have someone read aloud 1 Thessalonians 5:1-11. Form four groups, and assign each group one of these short passages: 1 Thessalonians 5:1-2, 3-4, 5-6 and 7-8. Distribute paper and markers or crayons and ask each group to draw a picture that illustrates its assigned passage. After a few minutes, have groups explain their drawings to the rest of the class. Ask:

● **What advice did Paul give in these verses?**

● **What piece of advice in these verses seems the most important in getting ready for Jesus' return? Explain.**

# ◆ Experience

Say: **All through the New Testament, Christians are encouraged to be ready for Christ's return. Jesus himself told a story to illustrate this important command.**

Read aloud the parable of the ten virgins found in Matthew 25:1-13. Then say: **Let's see how this parable might be different if it were written today.**

Form two teams and give each team a flashlight with no batteries. On the floor between the two teams, place two sets of batteries that fit the flashlights. One set should contain working batteries; the other set should contain dead batteries. Toss a coin to see which team gets first pick at the sets of batteries.

Once teams have chosen their batteries, turn off the lights and say: **Somewhere in the room I've hidden an excellent prize. Use your flashlight to find it.**

Allow kids to load their batteries into their flashlights and test them. When one team realizes its batteries are dead, have that team sit down and wait while the other team searches out the prize—a large bag of M&M's candies.

Once the prize is found, turn on the lights and allow the winning team to enjoy its treats.

# ◆ Grow

Ask:

● **Did you like this activity? Why or why not?**

● **How did it feel to be caught with dead batteries? to have live batteries?**

● **How is this like the parable we just read?**

● **How is this like being ready for Christ's return?**

● **What can we do in our lives to make sure our "batteries" are always ready to go?**

Say: **It's easy to forget Christ's promise to return and to live our lives as though he were never coming back. But his promise is real, and we can learn to build our lives around that truth so our readiness "batteries" never run down due to neglect.**

# ◆ Go

Give each person a sheet of paper and a pencil. Say: **Let's see how our lives might change if we knew Jesus was coming back really soon. If you suddenly found out that Jesus was coming back in exactly one year, what five things would you be sure to do before he returned?**

Allow a few minutes for kids to write, then say: **What if you learned that Christ was coming back in exactly one month? What five things would you be sure to do before he returned?**

Allow a minute for kids to write, then say: **What if you miraculously discovered that Christ was coming back in exactly one hour? What five things would you be sure to do before he returned?**

After kids write for another minute, have volunteers tell what they wrote for each section. Then ask:

● **If a friend of yours asked you what he or she needs to do to get ready for Jesus' return, what would you say?**

After discussing kids' responses, close with prayer, asking God to help kids reshape their lifestyles based on the truth of Christ's imminent return.

After the prayer, offer everyone a second bag of M&M's candies to enjoy together.

# Lead On!

## ◆ Theme: Youth Leadership

(1 Timothy 4:11-16; 2 Timothy 2:22-26)

Paul was Timothy's "spiritual dad." Paul nurtured the young man in his faith and watched him grow quickly into a mature man of God. So it was no surprise that when Paul needed help on one of his missionary journeys, he took Timothy with him. Likewise, when Paul started a new church in Ephesus and needed someone to lead it, he called on Timothy. Paul trusted Timothy's wisdom and challenged him to guard the doctrines that Paul had taught the church there.

There was only one hindrance to Timothy's leadership. Timothy was young. He wasn't always taken seriously by some in the church. But Paul did not allow Timothy to use that as an excuse to give up or compromise his stance. This session helps kids understand their role as leaders today, whatever their age.

## ◆ Objectives

During this session kids will:
● explore 1 Timothy 4:11-16 and 2 Timothy 2:22-26;
● identify risks of being a leader;
● compile a biblical "job description" for leadership; and
● test their own leadership skills.

## ◆ Preparation

Read and study 1 Timothy 4:11-16 and 2 Timothy 2:22-26.

Gather pencils, paper, Bibles, newsprint, markers, a stopwatch or watch with a second hand, and 3×5 cards.

# The Session

## ◆ Dig

Say: **I'm sorry, guys. I've had an exhausting day, and I just
don't have anything to offer you today. In the interest of my
own emotional health, I've decided you should plan and lead
the session today.**

Form groups of three and give each group a pencil, paper and
a Bible. Say: **All I can tell you is that we're supposed to study
1 Timothy 4:11-16 and 2 Timothy 2:22-26. Based on these passages, plan a meeting with at least three activities.**

Allow several minutes for groups to tackle the assignment.
Some will go at it enthusiastically, while others may feel over-
whelmed by the task. After several minutes, ask:

● **How does it feel to suddenly be in charge? Explain.**
● **What did you need that I didn't give you to do a good job?**
● **What are the risks of being a leader?**
● **How do you feel about kids being leaders?**

Say: **Even though my earlier instructions were just a setup,
the truth is that each of you is a leader right now in one way or
another. Today we're going to talk about what it means for you
to be a leader among your friends and family.**

## ◆ Discover

Say: **Timothy was a close friend of the Apostle Paul. He
traveled with Paul and probably knew Paul's methods and
goals as well as anyone. It should have been no surprise that
Paul appointed Timothy to lead churches Paul had begun. Still,
some people in the early church felt Timothy was too young to
be a leader. But Paul knew that, as far as God is concerned,
quality leadership can come from people of any age.**

Have kids stay in their trios. Say: **On the back of your papers
from the first activity, list as many leadership qualities as you
can find in 1 Timothy 4:11-16 and 2 Timothy 2:22-26. Take**

**three minutes, and let's see which group can pick out the most leadership qualities from these passages.**

After three minutes, have each group count and then read its list of leadership qualities.

Say: **Let's pretend we need to hire someone to be a leader, and we want to include biblical principles in our hiring. We need to decide what qualities we're looking for.**

Have the class select one person to be the "scribe" who will write the job description on newsprint. Encourage kids to suggest characteristics from the lists derived from the scripture passages. When the job description is complete, ask:

● **How would filling this job be tough for you?**

## ◆ Experience

Say: **It's easy to talk about leadership, but it's not as easy to be a leader. Right now each of us will have a turn at being a leader. Remember what we've talked about while we try this.**

Have the class line up single file. Say: **One at a time, I'm going to whisper a description of a different task in each person's ear. That person's job as a leader is to get the rest of the group to perform that task within one minute. There's only one rule: Leaders may make all the noise they want; however, they may not speak words.**

Whisper a task description from the list below into the first person's ear and have that person "lead" the rest of the group to perform the task. Once the task is accomplished, or the minute is up, move to the next person and the next task description. Continue until all the kids have had a chance. It's okay if a few kids get the same task.

Here's the list of task descriptions:
● Form a human pyramid.
● Spin around like a ballerina.
● Collect all the trash in the room into a pile.
● Bow three times to the north.
● Clap and sing "My Country 'Tis of Thee."
● Hop around on one foot in a circular pattern.
● Form a circle and bark like a dog.
● Give three different people a quick back rub.

- Run in place.
- Move the chairs into a square shape.

When all the kids have had a chance to lead, ask:

- **Did you enjoy this activity? Why or why not?**
- **How did you get people to do what you wanted?**
- **How is that like the way "real" leaders lead their groups? How is it different?**
- **What leadership qualities did you see most in our group?**
- **What leadership qualities do you think we could work on as a group, based on this exercise?**

Say: **All of us can be leaders. And not just in a game. We can be leaders in real life too—at home, at work, at church and at school.**

# ◆ Grow

Ask:

- **How can you be a leader at home? at work? at church? at school?**
- **What things get in the way of good leadership?**
- **How can we change those things?**
- **What do you personally need to change to let those good qualities we discussed come alive?**

# ◆ Go

Say: **The biggest part of being a leader is recognizing the leadership roles you already have and learning to be responsible in them. As you do, you'll find yourself growing in leadership in other areas too. Let's close today by deciding how we can be better leaders this week.**

Give each person a 3×5 card and a pencil. On their cards, have kids each write one way they can be more responsible leaders during the upcoming week at school, at home, at work or at church. When kids are finished, have volunteers tell what they wrote. Challenge kids to keep their cards with them during the upcoming week as reminders to be responsible leaders. Close with prayer, asking God to help kids be wise, responsible leaders.

# 27 Faith in Action

## ◆ Theme: Active Faith (James 2:14-26)

Faith is a wonderful thing to have. But, as James points out, faith without works is dead. While some churches might disagree with James' emphasis on works, most Christian leaders agree that faith and works are closely tied together.

This session helps teenagers see the importance of living out their faith in their daily lives.

## ◆ Objectives

During this session kids will:
- play volleyball two different ways to introduce the importance of taking action on their faith;
- discover how faith requires action;
- examine the risk of acting on beliefs; and
- commit to making their faith come alive.

## ◆ Preparation

Read and study James 2:14-26.

Gather a volleyball net, a beach ball, a bowl of water, a dry sponge, Bibles, a $1 bill or a $5 bill, 3×5 cards and pencils.

# The Session

## ◆ Dig

Set up a net for a game of volleyball. Use a large plastic ball or beach ball so kids who don't feel comfortable with sports can enjoy the game.

Form two teams and have them play for a few minutes just for fun, without keeping score. Then call one team over and secretly tell them not to try to hit the ball, but to talk among themselves as if they weren't playing a game at all.

After a few minutes of playing this way, call the group together and ask:

● **How did you feel when one team stopped trying to hit the ball?**

● **What important element was this team missing?**

● **How important is action in games like volleyball?**

Say: **Action is an important part of games such as volleyball, but it's an important part of our faith too.**

## ◆ Discover

Place a bowl of water on the floor. Give a small, dry sponge to a volunteer and ask him or her to use the sponge to cool off group members. But don't let the volunteer use the water. The volunteer will probably wave the sponge as a fan to cool people.

Then read aloud James 2:14-26.

Have another volunteer wet the sponge and use it to cool off group members by gently wiping their foreheads with the wet sponge.

Ask:

● **When did you feel "cooled off" the most in this activity?**

● **How's our dry sponge like faith without works?**

● **How's our wet sponge like faith with works?**

● **What's the key to James' message in this passage of scripture?**

Read aloud James 2:14-26 again, then say: **A sponge is made to hold water. Without water, it's practically useless for wiping up spills or cleaning. Similarly, our faith was made to be acted upon. Trusting in Christ makes us Christians, but we may be like dry sponges if we don't act on our faith.**

## ◆ Experience

(If you prefer, you can use a quarter instead of a $1 bill, and a $1 bill instead of a $5 bill in this activity.)

Say: **If you believe I can turn a $1 bill into something more valuable, come up and give me a $1 bill. I'll need to keep the dollar, though, so don't plan on getting it back.**

If no one takes you up on your request, ask:

● **Why didn't anyone take me up on this request?**

● **Why is it easy to say we believe something but hard to act on it?**

If someone gives you a dollar, put it in your pocket and say: **This person believed I could turn this dollar into something greater. And he (or she) is right.** Give that person your $5 bill.

Then ask:

● **How did you feel when I gave this person a $5 bill?**

● **What was different about what the volunteer did and what other people did?**

● **How is acting on my request like acting on your faith?**

● **How much risk is involved in acting on faith? Explain.**

## ◆ Grow

Ask:

● **What are specific ways we can live out our faith?**

Give each person a 3×5 card and a pencil. Say: **Choose five things you can do that James might refer to as "works"—things that show your faith in action. Some examples are helping an elderly lady with her shopping or telling a friend about your faith. List each thing you choose on your card.**

When kids are finished, have them each find a partner. Have partners tell each other what they wrote and how and when they'll carry out their plans.

**Go**

Say: **If we love God and want to serve him, we'll naturally act on our faith and live lives pleasing to God.**

Form a circle and have kids put their arms around each other in a group hug. In closing, pray: **Dear God, help us to make our faith more than words. Help us act on our love for you in all we do, that we might glorify you by our actions as well as our words. In Jesus' name, amen.**

# Counting the Cost

## ◆ Theme: The Cost of Discipleship
(1 Peter 4)

In this passage, Peter admonishes Christ's followers to follow through on their commitment to Jesus by accepting the cost of discipleship. Peter lived out his own teaching. He followed Jesus with his whole heart. In fact, tradition holds that Peter was crucified upside down because of his choice to follow Jesus.

This session helps kids understand the seriousness of a commitment to follow Christ and helps them "count the cost" in their own lives.

## ◆ Objectives

During this session kids will:
- try to construct a tower with insufficient supplies;
- list the costs of following Jesus found in 1 Peter 4;
- participate in a story that will cost them everything; and
- discover how they will be able to pay the price of being a disciple of Jesus.

## ◆ Preparation

Read and study 1 Peter 4. Gather a bag of bubble gum, a package of spaghetti, Bibles, pencils, tape, newsprint and markers. Make two photocopies of the "Disciple of Jesus Sales Ticket" (page 136). Also, photocopy and cut apart the "Cost Cards" (page 137) to use in the Experience section.

# The Session

## ◆ Dig

Form groups of three and give each group a piece of bubble gum and two strands of uncooked spaghetti. Tell groups to use their supplies to build a tower at least 3 feet high. Kids will soon begin to complain that they don't have enough spaghetti to build a tower that high, but just encourage them to do the best they can.

After a few minutes, have groups stop and ask if any group managed to complete its tower. Then ask:

● **How did it feel to find you didn't have enough supplies to complete your tower?**

● **How might we have avoided this problem?**

Read aloud Luke 14:27-30, then say: **Jesus compared building a tower to becoming his disciple. He warned people not to jump into becoming his disciples without first understanding how much it would cost them. Today we'll look at the cost of becoming a disciple of Jesus and discover whether we've really got what it takes.**

## ◆ Discover

Form two groups and give each group a pencil and a copy of the "Disciple of Jesus Sales Ticket" (page 136). Have each group look up the passage on the ticket and race against the other group to list the most things from the passage that could be considered a "cost" of being a disciple of Jesus. Allow about five minutes.

While kids are working, tape a sheet of newsprint to the wall and title it "The Cost of Discipleship." When time is up, have each group explain the costs it listed. Write the answers on the newsprint. When groups are finished, review the list and applaud the group that came up with the most costs.

Say: **We can already see that following Jesus costs a lot, but the cost is even greater than this passage indicates. Let's read a story to see what else it costs to become a disciple of Jesus.**

# ◆ Experience

Have kids form a semicircle of chairs then pass out the numbered "Cost Cards" you cut apart earlier. It's okay if some kids don't get a card or if some kids receive more than one. It will help you if you pass out the cards sequentially from left to right—that way you won't have to search for the location of the next card each time.

Explain to kids that you're going to read them a story that includes the sections printed on their cards. Tell the kids you'll cue each of them when it's time to read their part of the story.

Read aloud the "Parable of the Purchase" below, pausing where indicated to allow kids to read their cards. After each card is read, take it before continuing the story. By the end of the story, you should have all the cards back in your hand.

---

## PARABLE OF THE PURCHASE

Once upon a time, there was a teenager who loved diamonds. One day, he went into a jewelry store and saw in the display case a beautiful diamond—more beautiful than any he had seen before. In fact, he was so captivated by the beauty of this diamond that he decided to buy it.

The teenager asked the sales clerk how much the diamond cost.

"Oh, that's an expensive diamond, that is," said the sales clerk. "I'm not sure you have enough to buy it."

"How much is it?" persisted the young man.

"Well, that's hard to say exactly," said the sales clerk. "How much do you have?"

(Card 1)

"Let me see them," said the old sales clerk. When the teenager produced the money and the cards, the old man snatched them out of his hand. "Okay," he said. "That's a start. What else?"

"Huh?"

"What else do you have?"

"Well, nothing," said the young man.

"Oh come, come lad," said the old man. "You must have something else. Think."

(Card 2)

---

**132**

"Just what you've got on?" asked the man.

"No, I have a whole closetful at home," said the teenager.

"Oh, well that's good; I'll take them. What else? Think big now."

(Card 3)

"Your car. Yes, I'll take that too. Go on."

"You mean you want more?" asked the young man.

"It's a very expensive diamond," replied the old man with a grin. "What else?"

(Card 4)

"Oh, of course, we'll add those to the list. Keep going."

"That's all I have," said the young man, a little despondent.

"Nonsense," replied the old man. "You've got to have more assets than that. What about your personal abilities, your dreams and goals?"

(Card 5)

"Well, it's a good enough place to start, I reckon," said the clerk. "Do you spell 'career' with two r's in the middle?"

"You're going to take my career in exchange for the diamond?" asked the young man.

"Sure, sure. It's an expensive diamond," the old man reminded him. "In fact, I can see right now that to get this diamond, it's going to cost you all you have."

"I've already given you my career and all my possessions. What else can there be?" asked the teenager.

"Oh, we haven't even gotten to the really valuable things yet," said the man, his eyes twinkling. "Now, what about those goals I was talking about?"

(Card 6)

"There you go! Now that's worth something," said the old man. "Keep going, lad, you're on a roll."

"I can't think of anything else," said the young man.

"Oh, you can't, can you?" asked the man. "What's that you have there?"

"You mean this pen?"

"No, no, no," the old man smiled again. "What's holding the pen?"

(Card 7)

(Card 8)

(Card 9)

"Slow down, lad," said the man. "Okay, hands, ears and mouth, did you say?"

(Card 10)

"Oh, that's fine, then," said the old man. "Saves a bundle on the paperwork that way. Now, please, go on."

"More? You want more?"

"I told you it would cost you all you have," said the old man.

"What else is there?" exclaimed the teenager.

"Well, lad, the body's just a shell, after all," said the man. "The real valuable stuff is inside."

"You want my liver?"

"No, no," said the old clerk. "I got that with the body, remember? I was speaking of deeper things—thoughts and such."

(Card 11)

"Yes," said the man plainly. "And?"

(Card 12)

"Exactly," the clerk smiled. "And I'll just add in your will for good measure. Now, let's see. It looks like you have almost enough. Only a few things do you lack."

"I can't imagine what they might be," said the young man.

"Your relationships," said the old man. "Who do you know?"

(Card 13)

"Family, good."

(Card 14)

"Friendships. Uh-huh."

"That's it," said the teenager.

"You ever plan on getting married, lad?" asked the man.

(Card 15)

"Ah, yes. The kids put it just over the top. You've got just enough. The diamond is yours."

## ◆ Grow

After the story, ask:

● **Did you like that story? Why or why not?**

● **How does this story reflect the cost of becoming a disciple of Jesus?**

● **How did you feel as you read your card and I took it away?**

● **How is that like the cost of becoming a disciple of Jesus?**

● **How is it different?**

Say: **To become Christ's disciple we must give him everything in our lives. That doesn't mean we lose everything we have, such as our clothes or our friendships. It just means that we give up our control over those things and give that control to God.**

**Go**

Say: **The cost of becoming Christ's disciple seems high, doesn't it? Well, it is. It's so high, in fact, that we're probably all wondering whether anyone could ever pay such a price. Without God's help to strengthen us, we probably couldn't. But God promises to help us follow him faithfully if we just make the choice.**

Have kids return to the groups of three they formed at the beginning of the session. Tell groups once again to build a 3-foot tower of spaghetti, but this time supply them with far more spaghetti and bubble gum than they need. Encourage kids to be creative with their towers.

When everyone is finished, applaud each group's efforts then read aloud 2 Corinthians 9:8 and say: **The abundance of supplies you got this time is like the abundance of God's grace to help you continuously pay the price of being his disciple.**

Close with prayer, thanking God for calling kids to be his disciples.

# DISCIPLE OF JESUS

## SALES TICKET

### 1 Peter 4

_____      _____

_____      _____

_____      _____

_____      _____

_____      _____

_____      _____

_____      _____

_____      _____

_____      _____

_____      _____

                                Total     _____

# COST CARDS

## INSTRUCTIONS:
Photocopy and cut apart these cards to use in the Experience section.

**1.** "Well, I only have a few hundred dollars with me, but I have a MasterCard and a Visa."

**2.** "Well, I've got my clothes."

**3.** "My car?"

**4.** "Well, I have all my possessions."

**5.** "You mean my career?"

**6.** "You mean my future?"

**7.** "My hand? You mean my hands? You want my hands?"

**8.** "Good grief, mister! You might as well take my ears while you're at it!"

**9.** "And my mouth as well!"

**10.** "Oh, why not just finish the job and take my whole body?"

**11.** "You want my thoughts? You want my mind?"

**12.** "My . . . emotions?"

**13.** "Well, my family."

**14.** "And there are my friends."

**15.** "Yeah, I guess so . . . Okay, throw in my marriage and any kids I might have."

# Turn the Light On!

## ◆ Theme: Walking in God's Light
(1 John 1:5—2:11)

Have you ever wondered *why* God created light? He didn't have to. He could've created us so that we'd live by touch, sound or some other sense we don't have now. So why light?

First John gives us a strong clue as to God's reasons for creating light. All of God's creation is designed to reveal his character in some way. From 1 John we see that, possibly more than any other quality of creation, light seems to best represent God's nature and how he operates in our lives. Use this session to help kids understand how God is like light in our lives and to encourage them to walk in that light.

## ◆ Objectives
During this session kids will:
● list things that light is good for;
● discover how God and light are similar;
● experience walking in darkness; and
● make a commitment to walk in God's light.

## ◆ Preparation
Read and study 1 John 1:5—2:11.

Gather matches, paper, pencils, metal trash cans, Bibles, light bulbs, fine-point permanent markers and grocery sacks.

# The Session

## ◆ Dig

Form groups of four and give each group a match, paper and a pencil. Provide metal trash cans so kids can dispose of used matches safely. Assign one person in each group to be the scribe and say: **On "go," light your match and begin naming all the things light is good for before the match burns out. Go!**

When everyone is finished, have groups tell what they wrote. Then ask:

● **Did you run out of ideas before the match burned out?**

● **What are some other benefits of light that we haven't mentioned?**

● **Why is light so important to our lives?**

Say: **Light is crucial to life on earth isn't it? Today we're going to talk about a different kind of light that's just as crucial to our lives—God's light.**

## ◆ Discover

Have kids stay in their groups and give each group a Bible, a light bulb and a fine-point permanent marker. Have groups read 1 John 1:5—2:11, then list on their light bulbs ways that God and light are similar.

When groups are finished, have each explain its light bulb. Then ask:

● **Why is God's light in our lives so important?**

● **What happens when we don't have God's light?**

● **What do you think shuts God's light out of our lives?**

Say: **God's light is real and is always around us in this life. But the barriers that keep us from experiencing his light are just as real. Let's explore what those barriers are and how we can remove them.**

# ◆ Experience

Read 1 John 1:5-7 aloud. Say: **That's a powerful statement about darkness. Let's experience what it means.**

Give each person a sack and a marker. Say: **Inside your sack, write ways you sinned in the past week. Sin is anything that you do or think that displeases God—or even things you should do but don't. Be honest. For example, you might write that you made fun of someone at school or lied to your mom. Whatever comes to mind, write it down inside that sack.**

When kids finish, gather in a circle. Have kids place their sacks over their heads and try to shape their chairs into a square. After a few minutes, have kids sit down and take their sacks off.

# ◆ Grow

Ask:

● **How did you feel during this experience?**

● **How was walking around with the sack on your head like walking in darkness without God's light?**

● **Why did you bump into things?**

● **How is that like getting into bad situations in your life?**

● **How does sin keep us out of God's light?**

Read aloud 1 John 1:8-9. Say: **There's good news in that passage. We don't have to walk in darkness. God wants us to walk in the light. Through forgiveness we can experience God's power to live as we should.**

# ◆ Go

Have kids form a circle. Say: **Walking in God's light is a choice. As we learn to walk away from sin, we'll find ourselves living in the brightness of God's light. Let's close today by making a commitment to walk in God's light this week.**

On their sacks, have kids each complete this statement: "This week, I will walk in God's light by ... " When kids are finished, have volunteers tell what they wrote. Then close with prayer. After the prayer, challenge kids to take their sacks home and place them in their rooms as reminders to walk in the light of God.

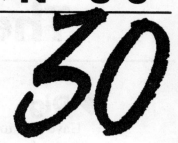

# The Power of Visions

## ◆ Theme: The "Big Picture" of Revelation (Revelation)

The book of Revelation has been explained in countless ways over the centuries. But to get a timeless message from it, we must look at the big picture behind it.

Simply stated, it is this: God wins. And he enables us to be winners too. Use this session to give kids hope for the victorious future that's already been determined by God.

## ◆ Objectives

During this session kids will:

- discuss what makes some dreams and visions important;
- represent the visions of Revelation through pipe-cleaner sculptures;
- create their own "movie titles" for Revelation; and
- thank God for assuring Christians of victory in the end.

## ◆ Preparation

Review Revelation and study the major visions John recorded in the book.

Gather Bibles, pipe cleaners, paper and pencils.

# The Session

## ◆ Dig

Have kids form a circle with their chairs. Say: **Scientists say everyone dreams but not all people remember their dreams. Did you ever have a dream you couldn't forget? Let's talk about what makes some dreams stick with us.**

Go around the circle and have kids each tell both the best dream they remember and their worst nightmare. Discuss what makes a dream good or bad. Ask:

● **Do you think dreams ever mean more than what they seem to mean on the surface? If so, how does that happen?**

● **What's the difference between a dream and a vision?**

## ◆ Discover

Say: **At times God has spoken to humans through dreams and visions. One such case is the book of Revelation, which is a series of visions seen by the Apostle John while he was a prisoner on the island of Patmos.**

Form pairs. Distribute Bibles and assign each pair one or more of these chapters from Revelation: 1 (verses 9-16); 4; 5; 10; 12; 15; 18; 19; and 22. After pairs have read their chapter(s), give each pair a pipe cleaner for each chapter they read and instruct them to make something that represents the content of the chapter(s). Then have pairs tell about their chapters and explain their sculptures. Ask:

● **Why do you think God used symbols in visions to communicate his message to John?**

Say: **We've made symbols out of pipe cleaners to represent the visions we read about. The symbols help us explain God's message to each other. The book of Revelation is full of symbols of its own. They may seem confusing at first, but they all work together to make a statement.**

# ◆ Experience

Say: **Sometimes it's easier to understand something if you take a look at the "big picture." Let's try that with the book of Revelation.**

Have kids huddle together in a tight circle. If your group is large, form small groups of at least eight. Once kids are huddled, have them each extend their right hand into the center of the huddle and randomly grab the hand of someone else in the circle. While still clasping right hands, have kids do the same thing with their left hands, making sure they don't grab hands with the person whose right hand they are already holding.

Once kids are tangled, ask:

● **How does it feel to be all knotted together? Explain.**

● **How is this like the abundance of symbols and visions contained in Revelation?**

● **Do you think we can take this jumbled mess and create something simple and ordered? Why or why not?**

Say: **Let's try. Without letting go of anyone's hand, work together to untangle your knot to reveal a circle.**

Give kids several minutes to untangle themselves without letting go of their handclasps.

# ◆ Grow

Once kids are untangled and a circle is formed, ask:

● **Did you think this was possible? Why or why not?**

● **How did you feel when you discovered you could untangle your knot?**

● **How is that like the way all the symbols and visions work together in Revelation?**

Say: **On the surface, the many visions and symbols contained in Revelation can seem confusing and jumbled. But once you unravel them a bit, you can see they all point toward one simple theme. Let's do one more activity to see what that theme is.**

**Go**

Give each person paper and a pencil and have them each make up a two- to five-word movie title that summarizes what all the visions together are saying to them. When kids are finished, have them tell what they wrote and why.

Say: **If the book of Revelation was a movie, I would title it something like "God Wins in the End." The overall message of Revelation is that God's victory over evil has already been decided. That's good news for those of us who walk with God because it means that, no matter what happens today or next week, we are destined to win in the end.**

Close with prayer, thanking God for revealing the certainty of our victory over evil in the book of Revelation.